COMPTIA NETWORK+

A Comprehensive Beginners Guide to Learn About The CompTIA Network+ Certification from A-Z

Walker Schmidt

Table of Contents

Introduction

If you are just getting into the world of certifications, you have made one of the best decisions of your life. Certifications open avenues for you to succeed in so many ways that you never would have imagined. By attaining a special certification, you stand a chance of getting selected for a position more than anyone else in the same category.

A certified expert is more valuable to the organization. There is a lot of study material that you will get through before you get certified. You will have to sit through exams to prove you have what it takes to make it in networking. One of the best things about Network+ certification is that everything you learn will be useful in your career.

This book helps you prepare for your exams, by reminding you some of the facts that you might have forgotten, or taken for granted. Your exam will feature multiple choice questions. This is the same style that you might have used back in school. Most students assume that multiple choice questions are easy, and this is the first mistake they make.

Much as multiple choice questions have the correct answers in front of you, you must think outside the box. Network + exams attempt to gauge your preparedness to tackle a real-life scenario. Because of this reason, you will encounter a lot of questions that go beyond cramming acronyms and facts, to addressing factual representation or application of the knowledge learned.

Once you go through this book, you have what it takes to get you through the introductory aspect of Network +. This book gives you the basics, the foundation upon which you can build on to pursue other critical certifications in networking.

Why do you need Network + certification? Just like you would for other certification programs like Oracle and Lotus, CompTIA Network + prepares you for the future by making sure that you are not just a skilled employee, but a skilled and duly certified employee. You become an important asset to whichever organization you are affiliated with.

While studying and preparing for your exams, you will notice that the questions often test different things. Do not just focus on answering the questions, but on skill and knowledge transfer. This is why you need a lot of practice before you are ready for an exam. Practicing often will help you look at the questions posed to you in an analytical capacity, and approach them from a problem-solving perspective.

Chapter One

Preparation Tips for
CompTIA Network+ Examination

CompTIA certification is mandatory for most of the top corporate jobs that involve networking or network security. With this certification, you have a better shot at an interview, and proving your worth in a hands-on capacity. Passing the exams is no mean feat either. Even some of the top professionals in the industry admit that this is one of the exams that gave them sleepless nights.

To prepare adequately for the exam, you must first understand what the exam structure looks like. You will be tested with multiple choice questions and performance-related questions. It is not easy to tell how many questions will come from either type, because each exam is set different from the last one.

The exam might be different all the time, but some useful tips that have helped many professionals succeed over the years will still apply today. Knowledge of these tips will help you smoothen the preparation process, and face the exam confidently. The following is a brief guide that will help you prepare for your CompTIA Network+ exam.

Understand performance-related questions

Performance questions demand that you carry out a specific task. The idea behind such questions is to determine whether you can use the knowledge gained to solve problems in a real scenario. If you can hack performance-based questions, there is a good chance you will perform well in the workplace. This is because you provide real solutions to real life problems in real time. Given that the nature of the business environment today demands more hands-on experience from employees, you can expect the focus of CompTIA Network+ examination in the near future to shift more towards a problem solving approach, hence an emphasis on performance-related questions.

Time management

Learn how to manage your time well. Do not spend more time on a question than necessary. If you cannot handle the question right away, mark it and get back to it later. Multiple choice questions should be easy for you to handle because you do not have to fill in the blanks or write an essay about the question. They are true or false questions, which means that the answer is already presented. The secret to hacking such questions is to familiarize yourself with the technical element of CompTIA Network+. Mastery of the knowledge jargon will go a long way.

Using CompTIA resources

When preparing for the CompTIA exam, make use of the resources available on their website. You will find these coming in handy as you prepare for the exam. Some of the useful resources include the list of acronyms and exam objectives. Familiarizing yourself with the list of acronyms makes your work easier when you come across relevant questions.

Building a network

Whether you are sitting for a CompTIA Network+ or A+, one of the most important things you must do is learn how to set up a network or a computer. It might seem like too much work at the beginning, but it is an important skill. Building your network from scratch helps you understand the critical elements in practice, and improve your mastery of the theoretical approach. It is easier to understand something that you create on your own than reading literature on something that someone else created.

Spare time for practice

CompTIA offers a lot of practice material that you can use when preparing for your CompTIA Network+ exam. From objective questions to practice tests, you have a lot of material to work with. One of the best ways of going about such material is to focus on the sections that you feel you struggle with.

Go over the sections that you constantly fail when revising or reviewing your answers. These are the ones where you must increase your effort to give you a better shot at passing the exam.

Vocabulary mastery

When preparing for or sitting in your exam, you must be careful about questions that contain words like *BEST, LEAST or MOST*. More often than not, all the answers provided are correct. However, you need to choose one that corresponds to the specificity of the question asked.

Learn from communities

There is a vibrant community of experts, professionals and students online. This is a community that will prove quite the resource when you are studying for your exam. Joining such a community is a good thing because of the wealth of experience available in there. Besides, the CompTIA exams are set based on the current curriculum, which addresses real-life scenarios. Why is this important?

Perhaps the study guide you have been using was written some years back, so in as much as you are ready for the exam, you might not be exposed to current affairs. From such a community, you will be well-versed with things that happen on a daily basis in the networking field, and you can also exchange ideas with the community members.

Plan for the exam

Think of the CompTIA Network+ exam like a marathon. You cannot start preparing for a marathon one week before the race day. Preparation takes months. The earlier you start preparing for the exam, the lighter your study or revision burden will be. You will have covered a lot of study areas by the time your exam date is due.

Starting early also allows you to create sufficient time to revise everything you have learned over time. You will also have noticed some of the sections that you believe are very difficult. For such areas, dedicate more time towards them so that you can understand them better.

Take advantage of related questions

You will often come across questions later on in the paper that can help you answer some that appeared towards the beginning. This is a common scenario that you should expect. Be steadfast in your answers. Otherwise, such questions can make you doubt your choices in the earlier question, and change a correct answer.

These questions, however, can also help you reflect and remember the correct answer, especially when the questions are related in some way. If you are ever in doubt, mark and skip the question and get back to it later.

Prepare adequately

While preparing for the exam, it is easy to get carried away and forget about pampering yourself. You need to be in the right frame of mind to pass this exam. First, make sure you are mentally prepared. Get sufficient rest, drink water, and eat properly before the exam. You want to walk into the exam room without a hint of stress.

Some people like to cram at the last minute before they get into the exam room. This might be effective, but it can also be counter-productive. The problem with last-minute cramming is that it is often a sign of ill-preparedness.

Know the location of your exam center, and make advance preparations if you are to travel to a different location. You do not want to be stuck in traffic, or held up at the airport because of airline delays and cancellations. If you are sitting for your exam in a new location, you must also allow enough time to familiarize yourself with the location, just in case you get lost in the process.

More importantly, remind yourself that you have come this far, and you have everything under control.

Types of Questions

There are different ways of testing you in a Network+ exam. When sitting for your certification exam, you will be tested on any of the following types of questions:

- **Multiple choice**

  Most of the questions in a Network+ certification are often multiple choice questions. The questions might have a single correct answer, or more than one correct answer for you to choose from. This is where your knowledge and application comes in handy. While some questions might ask you to choose the correct answer, some might ask you to choose all the answers that you feel are correct. You must, therefore make sure you think carefully before settling on an answer.

- **True or false**

  True or false questions are very easy. Each answer has a 50% chance of being right or wrong. You might not expect to find such questions in the certification exam. However, the questions can appear in a different format. You might be given a multiple choice question whose answers might be true or false. In this case, you have to deduce which of the answers you feel is appropriate for the question asked.

- **Graphical illustration**

  Graphical illustrations are used to emphasize a point. In class, you learn to use these illustrations to enhance your understanding of some concept. In a Network+ exam, these questions might be presented to clarify a question. You can be tested in the form of a network diagram or a set of pictures that represent a working network system. Some unique questions use the graphical illustration format to test your knowledge.

- **Free response**

  Free response questions are very rare in a Network+ exam. This is a question where you are expected to provide an answer in your own words.

Your preparedness for the job market

The Network+ examination tests, among other things, your ability to manage time effectively and perform tasks related to your work. Performance based questions will feature in your exam. However it might not be feasible for CompTIA to create an ideal laboratory situation where you can test your skills. The logistical cost of getting each candidate to the laboratory would not make sense.

Instead, CompTIA takes steps to make sure that they can test your preparedness for the job market in a different way. They create programs that will test your ability to accomplish certain tasks, and you are graded based on the same.

When sitting for a test, you launch a simulation program which operates the same way the real-life situation would. Simulations make the exam more realistic, and test you on things that are closer to problems you would encounter in a normal work environment.

One of the reasons why simulations are becoming popular is because they eliminate the risk of cheating in an exam. Everything you are expected to do is communicated in the test. It is impossible to cheat.

Chapter Two

Introduction to
Networks and Networking

One of the most important skills to help you pass a CompTIA Network+ exam is to understand how computers communicate with one another in a given environment. Other than passing the exam, this skill will also be useful to you as a networking expert when troubleshooting problems with the network in a work scenario.

In this chapter, you will go through a basic introduction to networks, the components, terminologies, and tips that form the basis upon which your knowledge of networking will be built. This chapter basically forms the foundation of your knowledge about CompTIA Network+.

Features of a network

Over the years, the cost of networking devices like home routers and hubs has become more affordable, and as a result a lot of people can and are creating small networks either at home or in their small offices. Today you can create a small network from your smartphone. As a certified Network+ expert, you must understand the relevant terminologies to help you master and offer support for such networks.

What is a network?

A network refers to a group of systems which are connected to one another for the sole purpose of sharing resources. Resources could be anything from printers to files. Resources could also refer to services, like an internet connection.

A network is built around two important features, software and hardware. Software is installed on the computers and devices within the network, allowing them to communicate effectively with one another. Hardware, on the other hand, refers to the physical machines and tools needed to complete the network.

Network hardware is composed of two important parts, the medium through which information is shared across the network, such as a wireless medium or cable, and the entities who need to share the resources and information across the network, such as workstations and servers.

Hosts, Workstations, and Servers

In a default simple network, the user has access to the workstation, through which they can access different applications, like a spreadsheet, email service, or word processor. In networking, the workstation is referred to as the **client**.

A workstation, therefore, is simply a computer running whichever operating system you install on it. When they access a workstation, users share files that are stored in the central server, with others on the network. The server is a unique, and special computer in the network that has more storage space and powerful memory than all the other computers. This computer is resource-intensive, hence the need to

11

make sure it is more powerful than all the other client workstations, to support the entire network.

Any computers or devices that connect to a network and communicate on the said network are known as hosts. A host, from this explanation, can be a printer, scanner, workstation, a server, a router, or any device that uses a network card.

LAN, MAN, WAN

While learning about networks, you will come across LAN *(Local area network)*, MAN *(Metropolitan area network)* and WAN *(Wide area network)* often. What is the difference between these network types?

LAN is a network type that is restricted to one building. It could be the network at home, in your office or your class in college.

WAN is a network type that covers several locations. WAN is basically a network of LANs. Take the example of a business that sets up multiple offices in different cities. To ensure that these offices all have access to the same set of information, each of their LANs would be connected to create a WAN.

MAN is a network type that only exists within a metropolitan area or a city. An example of a MAN is a situation where you have two buildings within the same town. These buildings would be connected together through a MAN.

Types of networks

There are different types of networks. Each organization or entity uses the network type that is suitable to their immediate needs. This is why you would find a learning institution running a different type of network compared to the local insurance company. There are basically two types of networks:

- Peer-to-peer networks

- Server-based networks

Peer-to-peer networks (P2P)

The term P2P is fairly common today, with many systems and applications using it to define the way they operate. A P2P network basically runs without a dedicated server. In place of a server, each of the workstations that are connected on the network share devices or information. The absence of a server in this network means that all the connected devices on a P2P network have and share equal access to network resources.

In a P2P network, each workstation assumes the double role of a server and client. A P2P network is often useful for small offices, homes, and personal networking needs, where it does not make financial sense to purchase a dedicated server, but at the same time, still fulfill the information and device sharing needs of staying connected to a network.

If you work in a small insurance firm that has only three computers, a P2P network would make sense. You can connect the computers to the printer and any other devices that you need to run the business on a daily basis. You can also share information about your insurance customers across the network. Such a set-up does not warrant the need for a dedicated server, which is often very expensive considering its computing resource requirements.

A typical P2P network should have no more than ten systems connected to it. If you use a Windows device, you will come across the term Workgroup, which is the connotation that Microsoft uses for a P2P network.

You will also notice that Windows operating systems like Windows 10 are designed to support P2P networking by default. The network settings are built-in, making your work easier. One of the challenges of this type of network is the fact that there is no central control or administration. Since each client on the network has equal rights, you must configure security features on each of them independently. You must also create user accounts for each of them.

Server-based networks

Server-based networks address one of the main challenges of running a P2P network, administration. Let's look at this from the perspective of a P2P network. You must create user accounts and set security privileges for each of them independently. One of the challenges with this is that you will end up with a situation where files are scattered all over the network. As a network administrator, you may have a very difficult time managing the network or the resources available to you.

While a P2P network should support up to ten devices, once you have more than four devices on the network, each of which are actively sharing information and acting as data stores, the need to have a central server becomes imminent. This is what a server-based network is all about.

In a server-based network, all the files and data are stored in one location; in the server, where everyone can access them. Because of this central location, a network administrator has an easier time managing resources because all you have to do is set permissions and unique parameters for accessing the files from the server, instead of doing so on each client on the network independently.

You also have a list of all the users on the server who have access to the network. A server-based network also makes work easier for backup and recovery in the event of data loss. The role of a server in this type of network depends on the services that you need. A server on such a network can offer different levels of utility, depending on the role it serves on the network. Some of these include:

- **File and print servers**

    The role of these servers is to manage the use of printers and files shared between clients on the network. A file and print server makes work easier in a situation where you have a lot of clients who need to access files and printers in the organization.

    File and print servers will often have any of the following features; very fast hard disks, large memory, redundant power supply, fast network adapters, fast input/output buses, and multiple CPUs.

- **Application servers**

    Application servers are unique as they are tasked with running a unique program on the server. They do not do anything else other than what they are intended to do. Some examples include the Microsoft SQL Server and an email server.

- **Web servers**

  Web servers are built to allow access to information on the internet. They specifically allow you to publish information online. They run HTTP (Hypertext Transfer Protocol). Web servers have become an indispensable part of the modern business environment because it is in them that web applications and websites are hosted. Web servers can host applications built for internal use (intranet) or information that is shared with the rest of the world on the internet.

- **Directory servers**

  Taking a hint from the name, a directory server contains a list of all user accounts granted permission to log into the network. The list is held within a database, referred to as the directory database. The database holds contact and identifier information about the user accounts, like the address, fax number, mobile phone number, and so forth.

  Managing a server-based network is easier because the directory server contains all the information about user accounts. If you connect to the network through any client, your sign in request is run through the directory server. Your client will only be allowed access to the network if the sign in credentials are recognized and accepted.

  It is also important to mention that one server can assume multiple roles instantaneously. You can use the same server as an application server, file and print server or directory server at the same time. Given this consideration, you do not need to worry about buying a new server whenever you add a new feature or implement something new on the network.

Extranet, Internet, and Intranet

The terms extranet, internet and intranet are used to explain the type of applications you use. You, therefore, need to know how to identify and tell them apart.

The *Internet* is used to share information with the rest of the world. To do this, you need an internet-type application that runs on SMTP, FTP, or HTTP. These are internet protocols that are available all over the world.

The *Intranet* is confined to a company. It is an internal network that cannot be accessed by anyone else outside the company parameters. Applications connect to the intranet through FTP or HTTP. Any information on the company intranet is inaccessible to anyone outside the company. While the information on the intranet might be accessible on a web browser, it is an internal network and you would not be able to access it outside the company network.

The *Extranet* refers to a situation where an application is designed for use by internal company employees through the intranet, but must also be accessed by a select group of customers or business partners. The extranet, therefore, is a situation where access to the intranet is extended to select individuals outside the company.

Chapter Three

Components of a Network

It is important to know what makes up a local area network. From network routers, switches, hubs to network cards, all these are important components that make up the network, the knowledge of which will not just help you in passing your Network + exam, but also help you as you go about tasks in the workplace.

A lot of the conventions related to networking computers and systems still remain the same as they were since the 1980s. However, what might have advanced is the processes and procedures. Technologies and systems have evolved in response to changes in computing and the need to make the number of connections you need to your computers as minimal as possible.

One thing that most users look forward to is fast, error-free communication, hence some of the changes that we have experienced over the years. All technologies depend on some form of physical media. Even wireless technology relies on some physical interface somewhere to make it effective. Most of the LANs you come across today are connected through cables. There are three types of cables used for networking today:

- Coaxial cables

- Twisted pair cables

- Fiber optic cables

Coaxial cables

A coaxial cable, also known as a coax has a central conductor built from copper, enclosed in a plastic jacket. The entire cable is shielded by a braiding. The shield is covered by PVC (polyvinyl chloride) or FEP (fluoroethylene propylene). Cables covered by FEP are often Teflon-type, also known as plenum-rated coating. Plenum-rated coating is very expensive, but is preferred because it meets the local fire standards especially when the cabling is passed behind walls or through the ceiling.

Twisted pair cables

Twisted pair cables are made up of several cables insulated individually, then twisted together to form pairs. In some cases, they are covered by a metallic shield, and referred to as *shielded twisted pair (STP)*. A twisted pair cable without the shield is referred to as an *unshielded twisted pair (UTP)*. These cables are commonly used for ethernet cabling.

There are different descriptions that are used for ethernet cables, each of which has a code. The code for ethernet cables is written in the format below:

$$N<Signaling>-X$$

Where,

N – signaling rate measured in megabits/second.

<Signaling> - the type of signaling, either broadband or baseband.

X – unique ethernet cabling scheme identifier

Why is it important that all the wires used for such cables are twisted? Electromagnetic waves on copper wires can cause interference when the wires are close to one another. This is called crosstalk. Twisting the wires, therefore, reduces the risk of this interference, and apart from that, protects the cables from interference from external sources.

Other than that, twisted pair cables are also preferred because they are very easy to work with, are more affordable than most of the other cabling types, and allow fast communication. Unshielded twisted pair cables are classified as follows:

- **Category 1** – Made of two twisted pairs, and is preferred for voice communication. It is limited to 1MHz frequency.

- **Category 2** – Made of four twisted pairs, with a frequency limit of 10 MHz, and can transfer data up to 4Mbps.

- **Category 3** – Made of four twisted pairs, with three twists after each foot of cable. It is limited to 16 MHz, and can support up to 10Mbps.

- **Category 4** – Made of four twisted pairs, with a frequency limit of 20MHz.

- **Category 5** – Made of four twisted pairs, with a frequency limit of 100MHz

- **Category 5e** – Made of four twisted wires, rated up to 100MHz. One of the main differences between Category 5 and 5e is that this can transmit on each of the four pairs at the same time, without any disturbance. This is a prerequisite for Gigabit Ethernet.

- **Category 6** – Made of four twisted wires, and rated up to 250 MHz.

At the moment, any classification that precedes 5e is either redundant or obsolete in the modern networking environment.

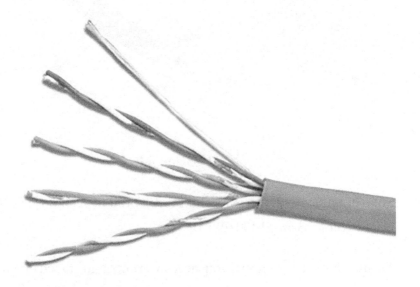

Category 5e cable

Source: https://www.cables.co.za/utp-cat5e-cable.html

It is very difficult to fit BNC connectors to a UTP cable. To solve this problem, you can use a registered jack connector (RJ).UTP cables use RJ-11 cables in case the device uses four wires, or RJ-45 if the device uses four pairs.

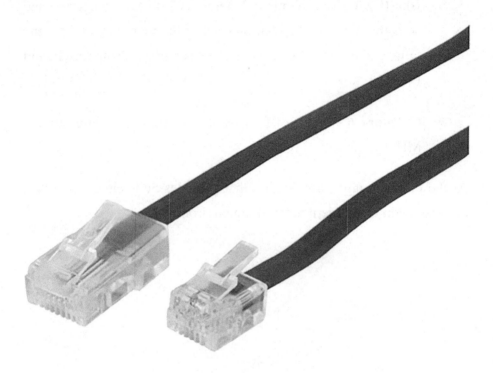

RJ-45 and RJ-11

Source: https://www.leroymerlin.fr/v3/p/produits/cable-rj45-rj11-male-male-evology-3-m-e1400149619

To use these connectors, you need a crimper to attach them to your UTP, in the same way you would for BNC connectors. While the die that holds the connectors might have a different shape for UTP connectors as compared to BNC connectors, today you have quality crimping tools whose dies are interchangeable, and can be used for either type of cable.

You will come across RJ-45 in many LAN connections. RJ-11s, on the other hand, are common in digital subscriber link (DSL) connections.

Fiber optic cables

While most of the cables transmit signals through electricity, fiber optic cables transmit signals through light impulses. This mode of transmission is preferred because the cables are immune to interference from RFI and EMI.

Fiber optic cables transmit the light impulses through plastic or glass cores. While glass is ideal because it allows transmission over a wider distance, plastic is preferred in most cases because it is affordable.

Whichever the core that is used for fiber optic cables, it is still protected inside a plastic or glass cladding with a different refraction index from the core, which helps to bounce the light back within the core.

Fiber optic cables are either multimode fiber (MMF) or single-mode fiber (SMF). The two modes are differentiated by the number of signals that they can transport. While SMF is preferred for long distance transmission, MMF is ideal for applications that require transmission over a short distance.

Fiber optic cables might have been touted as the next best thing since sliced bread, but it does have its pros and cons too. While fiber optic can transmit information up to 40 kilometers and is safe from interference through RFI or EMI, it is one of the most expensive cabling methods, especially when compared to twisted pair cabling.

Fiber optic cable installation is also not an easy process. The cost of repair or troubleshooting is also very high compared to twisted pair cabling. Another challenge for using fiber optic cables is that troubleshooting problems is not easy.

SMF uses laser and LED to transmit and carry the signals over a long distance. To enable communication, the source of light is pulsed through the cable. SMF cables can transmit data at a faster rate compared to MMF, and at a distance more than 40 times.

MMF, on the other hand, uses light for transmission, but instead of pulsing it through, it is reflected through the core from different paths upon which it is dispersed. To focus the light back into the core, the core is lined with a special cladding.

MMF is ideal for high speed bandwidth in medium range of around 2,000-3,000 feet. Anything more than this can introduce inconsistencies in transmission. Therefore, this also explains why MMF is preferred for connections that run within one building, while SMF is ideal for connections that run across multiple buildings.

SMF is primarily available in glass core, making installation quite a challenge. Other than that, it must never be pinched or crimped to circumvent a tight corner. MMF, on the other hand, is available both in glass and plastic. Installation is relatively easier especially with plastic, which makes it a more flexible solution.

Serial cables
Serial in networking refers to a scenario where one bit is transmitted after another through the connecting cable, and the communication is interpreted at the end where it terminates either on a NIC or a different

interface. There are several types of serial cables. Recommended Standard 232, *(RS-232)* is often used to connect data communications and terminal equipment together. Most devices today do not have RS-232 connectors, and instead, they have been replaced by FireWire and USB connectors.

USB is the ultimate connector built into most motherboards today. There is an endless list of devices that you can connect to a computer through the USB port. While most devices come with a maximum of 4 external USB slots, you can get an adapter. Most adapters max out at 16 interfaces. By design, USB can support connections of up to 127 external devices.

Characteristics of cables

Considering the different types of cables that can be used on a network, what are the unique properties that you should follow when choosing a specific cable over the others? The following are the main features that you must consider:

- **Frequency**

    Cables have a set frequency within which they can transmit bandwidth. Category 5e cables, for example, can transmit up to 100MHz, and at the same time, can also transmit up to 1Gbps over moderate distances.

    A category 6 cable, on the other hand, can max out at 250MHz, and will handle 1Gbps without any challenges. Considering that category 6 cables feature thicker cables and more twists, they are ideal for connections between different floors in a multi-story building.

- **Immunity**

A magnetic current is formed whenever electrons travel through two adjacent wires. This current is a good thing because it creates a magnetic flux. Magnetic flux is necessary to power the computers we use. However the power that surges through this current also brings forth a few concerns.

First, since the wires are generating current, anyone who has the right equipment can intercept the message without interfering with the wires physically. This creates a security issue. Some of the high profile establishments protect their installations by casing the communication wires within lead shielding.

Second, wires have the potential to adopt any current from around if they are anywhere near a magnetic source. Therefore, it is advisable to keep all wires as far away from strong magnetic sources like speakers, motors and amplifiers, to avoid EMI.

- **Distance**

The distance between the key components of any network will also help you determine the type of cable you need. While some cables can run further than others without glitches in communication, all networks will suffer attenuation at some point. Attenuation is signal degradation as a result of the distance the signal must travel, or the communication medium.

- **Duplex**

A communication platform can either be full duplex or half duplex. In half duplex communication, the device can either receive or send communication in one instant, but never both. This works like a walkie-talkie.

Full duplex communication, on the other hand, is a situation where the devices can send and receive communication instantaneously. Full duplex doubles the effective throughput, and as a result, makes communication highly efficient.

- **Transmission speed**

Network administrators can manage the network speed depending on the type of network and cable or fiber, to ensure that the network meets the traffic demand. Most administrators apportion maximum speeds in the core areas of the network, up to 10Gbps, and allow up to 10Mbps in segments where the network connects to switches, especially for basic access and distribution areas.

Chapter Four

Networking Devices

B y now, you must be well aware of most of the network connections and media that you come across from time to time. These connections originate or terminate in certain devices. The devices are referred to as connectivity devices because they connect to some network entity. In this chapter, we will discuss as many of the networking devices that you might come across as possible.

Hubs

The hub is a device where all the elements of an ethernet network are connected. Each device is connected to the hub through a cable. Through the hub, devices can connect to one another without segmenting the network. Any form of communication from a device is sent out to all the parts that are connected to the hub. This is to make sure that the CSMA/CD (carrier sense multiple access with collision detection) can assess the transmission for any collisions.

Source: https://www.amazon.com/D-Link-including-Charging-Adapter-DUB-H7/dp/B0000B0DL7

The role of a hub, therefore, is to ensure that all devices connected to the hub receive the same information. However, not all the devices will listen to the information. Only the device intended to receive the information can listen to it, according to the address in the information frame.

While hubs are useful, they have some challenges that are rendering them obsolete especially in corporate environments. Hubs broadcast communication from one device to all the other devices that it hosts. As a result, there is always a risk of collision, hence hubs are notorious for network collisions in any LAN with a lot of users.

Modem

The role of a modem is to modulate digital data to analog carriers, allowing transmission over an analog medium. Upon termination, the data is then demodulated to a digital signal for the recipient. Other than the description, a modem is actually no more than an acronym for *Modulator/Demodulator*.

There are three types of modems you might have come across today:

- **Cable**

  Cable modems are popular because they offer high speed technology for internet access. Through cable modems, you can connect any device to the internet, especially a network or an individual computer using the TV cable. Most TV companies today use the pre-existing cable infrastructure to offer their clients data services on the frequency bands that are not utilized. Cable modems feature a simple build. They come with an ethernet port and a coax connector at the rear end.

- **DSL**

  The digital subscriber line (DSL) is preferred over the conventional modem because it is an affordable way to offer high data throughput. One of the benefits of using DSL is that you can still access your regular calls online.

- **Traditional modems**

  A traditional modem, (plain old telephone service – POTS line) converts your computer signals into a package that can be transmitted through POTS. Most of the modems in use today are POTS because computer manufacturers have them embedded into the device motherboards.

Repeater

Repeaters are not so different from hubs. They can also be used to connect UTP connectors, adding your ethernet segment a 100-meter gain. It is not advisable to use repeaters in networks, however, because of latency. If you can, you can use a wireless network instead of a repeater without worrying about adding latency to the connection or losing bandwidth in the process. The same applies to hubs.

Basic router

A router is a networking device that allows you to connect several network segments together, in the process creating an internetwork. Routers can be intelligent, programmed to determine the most efficient way of networking and transmitting data to the destination. Such intelligent routers make decisions based on information gathered over time about the data performance on the network.

You are conversant with a normal SOHO (small office, home office) router. A SOHO router allows host connection to the internet through wireless or wired connection without additional configuration. These routers come with default configurations which you can use, but it is advisable to change them to personalized and secure credentials. Anyone can access the default access credentials for your router online if they know the make or model.

Source: https://www.harveynorman.com.au/dlink-ac1200-unified-wireless-router.html

Some routers are very complex, and come complete with their unique operating system. This is something you will find especially with Cisco routers, that run the Cisco IOS. Such routers have a CPU to help them process and route data packets efficiently and in a secure manner.

Given that such networks are intelligent, they can be programmed to perform other duties that you would expect of unique devices on your network, like firewall services. To do this, you activate or implement a given feature that is already built into their firmware.

Switch

A switch is just as common a component in a modern network as hubs are. The average user can confuse a switch for a hub. However, there are distinct features that tell them apart. Switches recognize the originator and destination MAC addresses for each frame, and the ports where the frames are delivered, while hubs cannot do that. Hubs simply send everything they receive to all devices that are connected to them.

Source: https://www.ebuyer.com/704518-netgear-gs108e-prosafe-plus-8-port-gigabit-ethernet-switch-gs108e-300uks

Bridge

The role of a network bridge is to connect similar segments of a network together. The idea behind this separation is to prevent domain collision within the network by separating traffic on both sides of the bridge.

When a bridge is used, traffic can only pass through it if the transmitter intends the transmission to be received on the other side of the bridge. A bridge comes in handy if you need to separate a very busy network into two segments and manage traffic accordingly. Bridges and switches use similar bridging parameters, though bridges run as software.

Network cards

Network cards are also known as network interface cards (NIC). The role of a network card is to enable your system to communicate with other devices on the network, by sending and receiving data. The NIC converts data into electronic signals which are then conveyed through electronic media, and into a format that the system can recognize. NIC provides electronic, electrical and physical connections between your device and other networked media.

You will also come across the NIC referred to as a network adapter. Most devices today come with the NIC pre-installed into the system. However, for older machines, you can purchase the adapter and install it into the system. A device that comes with the NIC pre-installed has an integrated network card. The network card is embedded into the system's motherboard.

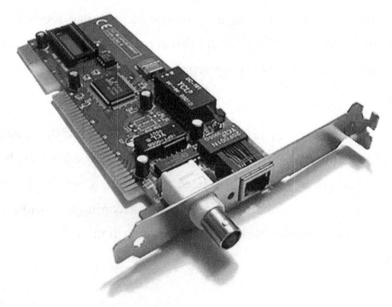

Source:
https://en.wikipedia.org/wiki/Network_interface_controller#/media/Fil
e:Network_card.jpg

For laptop computers, the NIC is often located on one of the sides, and at the back for most desktop computers.

For NICs that can be used as add-ons, you can plug them into the device through the USB drive, or through the expansion bus available on the computer. There are so many expansion slots that can be built into a computer. Your task is to make sure the expansion slot and the network card are compatible.

The following are some of the common expansion slots that you might come across:

- PCI

- AGP

- PCMCIA

- ISA

- EISA

- VESA

- MCA

By design, a PCI card is not compatible with an MCA slot, and so forth. You must match the card type and the expansion slots.

Transceivers

From the nomenclature, you can already sense a transceiver has something to do with communication. It is one of the network components that is tasked with receiving and transmitting signals across different media. The transceiver picks up signals and affirms that they do belong to the local system. A transceiver is also known as a media converter.

In case the data does not belong to that system, the transceiver discards it. However, if it belongs to the system, it is passed along for processing. You can either have an external or an onboard transceiver. The transceiver allows your NIC or any other device for that matter, to connect to a different media type that it was not built to connect to.

An onboard transceiver is built into the NIC, with the media connector located at the back of the network adapter. Common onboard transceivers include the BNC connector and RJ-45.

An external transceiver is one where the media connection is external. To connect a media device to this transceiver, you must attach an extension cable to the NIC. You need attachment unit interfaces (AUI) to use an external transceiver. The AUI is also referred to as the Digital Intel Xerox (DIX) connector. Each NIC can only work with a specific media and transceiver, depending on its connector.

A standard ethernet coax, also referred to as a thicknet, employs a connection method where you connect the external transceiver to the AUI of your NIC. The transceiver connects to the media attached to it through a vampire tap. A vampire tap is a connection where a hole is drilled into the cable without interfering with the central conductor.

The vampire tap might be effective, but it has its own challenges. It is largely obsolete today because of the difficulty in positioning the vampire tap properly such that it connects to the conductor without interfering with the surroundings. Other than that, the ethernet coax is also hindered by factors like very high cost and its size. While it might not be common in modern installations, you might come across it in some of the pre-existing installations from time to time.

Wireless access point

A wireless access point (AP) enables users on mobile devices to connect to a wired network through radio frequency technology. By design, a wireless access point is basically a wireless switch or hub because it allows you to connect several devices together and create a network.

Wireless access points are commonly used to offer internet access to users in public spaces like the airport, hotels, cafés and libraries. Wireless access points are relatively easy to set up. Setting up is as simple as connecting them to a wired network, turning on power and you are good to go.

Source: https://www.cisco.com/c/en/us/products/wireless/small-business-500-series-wireless-access-points/index.html

For a small business network, a wireless access point would be perfect because it is affordable, and takes away the challenge of expensive cabling.

Dynamic host configuration protocol server

A dynamic host configuration protocol server (DHCP) assigns each host an IP address. It makes work easier for network administrators because instead of static IP addressing, it automatically provides IP information. Static addressing is a situation where you assign each host an IP address manually.

DHCP servers are efficient in any networking environment irrespective of the size, and when in use, any hardware can be used as a DHCP server, even your router.

Firewall

A firewall is a security guard for your network. This is one of the most important things that you must always make sure is running on any network. Without a firewall, all communication on that network is accessible to anyone who can come across it.

Considering that almost all devices in use today are connected to the internet in one way or the other, there are so many intruders who look for unprotected networks. Someone who has unwarranted access to your network can use it and your devices for anything, including terrorism. They can also prevent you from accessing some important aspects of the internet.

Firewalls can either be software firewalls that are installed in a router or server, or you can also have a black box firewall. All firewalls must have at least two network connections. One connects the network (a private side) and the other connects to the internet (a public side).

You can also have an additional firewall which connects equipment and servers which might be deemed both private and public. A firewall is an important part of your network because it is your first line of defense especially if your network is connected to the internet.

Intrusion Detection or Prevention System (IDS/IPS)

IDS is a security tool deployed to detect any tactics that might be used by hackers to exploit your network. IDS detects network attacks, attacks on your network resources, applications and services. It also detects the presence of trojans, worms and viruses. However, IDS will only identify, detect and report such exploits. To stop the attack in question, you need IPS.

An IPS stays vigilant to protect your network from evil exploits. An IPS will monitor traffic to and from your network, search for any form of attack, including malicious code. When identified, IPS drops such compromised data packets, while at the same time allowing you to proceed with proper network use without any interference.

While IDS will only identify and report a potential threat, IPS will stop it, drop compromised packets, or shut down the port.

Domain name server (DNS)

One of the most critical servers in your network is the DNS server. DNS is also an important part of the internet. Each website address is identified by a unique address, such as http://206.124.115.189. It is impossible to remember all these digits. However, DNS allows you to enter the website as www.yourname.com. What this means, therefore, is that DNS is your phonebook to the internet.

Any device with an assigned IP address has a host name on the internet. This host name is part of what is referred to as a fully qualified domain name (FQDN). Each FQDN has a domain name and a host name.

Name resolution is the process through which you find the IP address for whichever host name. A name resolution can be performed in one of many ways, including the DNS. Domains are given a hierarchical structure on the internet, with the following considered some of the top-level domains:

- .com – for commercial organizations

- .gov – for government branches in the US

- .edu – for an educational institution

- .org – for non-profit organizations

- .net – for a network institution

- .mil – for the US military

- .int – for an international body like the UN

While these are the traditional top-level domains, other domains have come up over the years, and are equally important. These include:

- .me

- .biz

- .post

- .travel

- .cc

- .arts

- .info

Segmenting networks

When managing a large network, over time it becomes apparent that you need to break it into smaller segments that are easier to manage, and are efficient on resource consumption. More often this need arises because you have too many users on the network, slowing it down. Traffic congestion is one of the worst nightmares for any networking expert. Traffic congestion can be caused by any of the following:

- Low bandwidth, or exceeding your allocated bandwidth

- Using unnecessary hubs in the network for connectivity

- Multicasting

- Broadcasting storms

- Having too many hosts within the broadcast domain

If you encounter any of these challenges, consider splicing the network into smaller segments (network segmentation). You can segment a network by using a network switch or a router.

The hubs extend the collision domain from the main switch. Remember that you are still using one network (broadcast domain).

It is important to consider breaking up a network domain because whenever a server or host sends a broadcast, each device within the network has to access and process it, unless you are using a router.

Chapter Five

Open Systems Interconnection Model - OSI

The open systems interconnection model forms the foundation of your knowledge in networking. It is composed of seven layers, each of which plays an important role in determining effective and efficient communication between systems.

Earlier on, computers could only communicate with other computers from the same manufacturer. This means that if you had an Acer, you were unable to communicate with someone who was using an IBM, for example. OSI was developed late in the 1970s by the International Organization for Standardization (ISO) to help overcome some of the challenges that made communication impossible.

The concept of OSI was to make sure that network devices became interoperable. As a result, users on different networks were able to communicate with one another without any challenges. While some of the goals of implementing OSI have been met, some challenges still exist, which can be improved upon over time.

Networks, as we know them today, are built around the OSI model. OSI forms the foundational architecture for networks. By understanding how the OSI model works, you have knowledge of how information is transferred from one application through a network to a specific application on the other end. All this is achieved through a layered system.

Layered communication

The OSI model is a reference model. A reference model is simply a concept of how you expect communication to happen. This is a blueprint that shows all the procedures and processes that must be met for communication to take place between the components involved. These processes in the OSI are clustered into layers. Any communication network or system that is designed according to this method is referred to as a layered model.

Reference models are used by developers to help them understand how computers operate and communicate on a network. They also help developers understand the functions that must be met in each layer for smooth communication to take place. What this means is that if a developer is tasked with working on a protocol for a specific layer, they only need to focus on that layer, and not the others. Everyone is tasked with unique roles in building this network.

Importance of using reference models

While there are many reasons why reference models, and in particular the OSI model is useful in communication, the primary objective was to allow interoperability across vendor networks. Other than this, the layered model enjoys commendation for the following reasons:

- In this model, changes that take place in one layer are restricted to that layer alone. They cannot affect any other layer. For this reason, application development and the work of developers is much easier because they only need to focus on the layer they are tasked with.

- A reference model allows different software and hardware to communicate on the network without any encumbrances.

- By defining the functions and tasks that must take place in each level, layering supports standardization in the networking industry.

- Since network components are standardized, this reference model allows vendors to focus on developing reliable and efficient network components.

- The OSI model classifies communication processes in the network into small segments that are easy to manage, making work easier for network administrators and other associated experts during troubleshooting, design and development of unique network components.

OSI reference model

The OSI reference model is useful in that it helps you transfer data between dissimilar hosts. In this regard, you can transfer data from a Mac computer to a PC. The OSI model is a set of guidelines that developers use in a network. The OSI model comprises seven layers as follows:

- Application

- Presentation

- Session

- Transport

- Network

- Data link

- Physical

The application, presentation, and session layers determine the process of communication between applications and the end users. The rest of the layers are concerned with data transfer from one end of the model to the other. The upper layer that addresses communication between the user and applications is heavily leveraged on user interface. The bottom layer, on the other hand, is about network addresses.

Application

This is the first point of contact between users and the device. When the user interfaces with this layer, an expectation of a network access is apparent. A web browser, for example, processes requests by first interacting with the application layer. The application layer, therefore, is the interface of communication between the user and the next layer. Information is passed down from here to process user requests. The web browser in our example, is not a part of the application layer. It is only an interface that interacts with the protocols in the application layer to request access to resources that the user needs.

Another role of the application layer is to ensure the requested communication is identified, and establish its reliability. In this regard, the application layer will determine whether the network has enough resources to meet the needs of the user as keyed in through the interface.

Why is this important?

Computing demands unique resources, at times more resources than the user is aware. Other than the desktop resources, you might need other components of the network, and from more than one application. The application layer therefore, makes sure that all the necessary components are available.

Presentation

The presentation layer is about purpose. It sends data back to the application layer. The presentation layer is primarily tasked with formatting code and translating data. It is therefore the translator that stands between the user and the application. It codes and converts requests from the user to a language that the network understands, and sends back feedback to the user in responses that they understand.

The average user does not know a thing about computing languages. The presentation layer therefore, converts data to a native format that the user can read, something like ASCII. Other than that, the presentation layer also makes sure that any data that is transferred from the application layer of one system is understood by the application layer of another system to which a response is intended.

It is also in the presentation layer that services like encryption and decryption, compression and decompression are carried out. Whenever you use your device to access any media device, you enjoy the viewing or listening experience because of the presentation layer.

Session

The presentation layer has several sessions running from time to time, passing information from one layer to another. The role of the session layer is to manage these sessions accordingly. Nodes or devices that must communicate to process user requests are managed in the session layer because it provides the relevant dialogue control to support this communication.

You have come across communication modes like simplex, full duplex, and half duplex. These modes are organized in the session layer. In the simplest terms, the session layer makes sure that data from each application is separate from data from other applications.

Transport

The role of the transport layer is self-explanatory. It assembles data and packages it into a stream. The transport layer receives information from the upper layers, compacts it and pushes it along to the next layer in the data stream.

This layer checks to make sure there is a stable connection between the destination and originating host, and offers data transport services from one end of the spectrum to the other. It is also tasked with establishing a communication session, and tearing down a virtual circuit once communication has been completed.

The transport layer is built on transparency in data transfer. With this in mind, any information that is network dependent is hidden away from the top layer. It is in this layer that you will come across TCP and UDP. TCP, as you might already know, is a reliable service while UDP cannot be relied upon. Everything that happens in the transport layer comes down to the app or program developer. It is up to them to decide which mode they prefer between TCP or UDP for transport services.

Network

The role of the network layer is to make sure data can be transferred without a hitch. To do this, it manages addresses on the network, identifies where all the devices are located, and from that, establishes the most feasible way of moving data on the network. This layer ensures that data can be transferred between devices that are not directly connected to one another.

Routers play an important role in the network layer. They allow you to network devices together and share data across them. The router interface receives the data packets, then checks to confirm the IP address of the destination device. The router then sends the data packets to the right interface, where it is framed and forwarded to the correct LAN. If for some reason the router cannot find the destination network for the data packets in its routing table, it drops the data packets.

The network layer uses two types of packets:

- **Data packets**

  Data packets help in moving data all through the network. Any protocol that supports this is known as a routed protocol. Common routed protocols you might have come across include IPv6 and IP.

- **Route update packets**

  These packets make sure the connected routers are always updated about the networks they are connected to. They update the routers frequently. The role of these packets is to make sure that every router has an updated routing table for every other router on that network.

- **Interface**

  The interface refers to the exit point the data packets will use when dispatched to the destination network.

- **Network address**

  Network addresses are specific to the protocols. Each router must keep the routing table for each routing protocol because these protocols help in identifying the address schemes. You can think of this like a menu but in all the possible languages spoken by everyone who comes to that restaurant.

- **Metrics**

  Metric refers to the distance between the host network and the remote network. Every single protocol has a unique way of determining the distance.

Data link

The data link layer allows transmission of data. It is also the layer that handles error notifications. This layer makes sure that messages sent on the network are delivered to the right host device on the network.

How does this happen?

Messages shared on the network are converted into data frames, tiny bits of information. It also assigns a custom data header which includes the hardware address of the originating device, and the destination.

Routers within the network layer are not focused on the location of a host. Instead, their concern is on the location of the networks, and the most efficient way of getting to them. The data link layer identifies all the devices that belong to a network.

Remember that the data packets are not interfered with when they are transported. Instead, they are enclosed in the information that allows it to be transported to the relevant media type.

Physical

The physical layer is responsible for two important functions, sending and receiving bits. This layer determines the appropriate requirements for managing a physical link between two devices at different end points in the communication cycle.

The physical layer also has unique physical topologies and connectors, and it is for this reason that disparate systems can communicate with one another.

Chapter Six

Internet Protocol

To understand the internet protocol (IP), we must mirror the earlier discussions we had about TCP/IP. Knowledge of TCP/IP is important to understanding how the internet works. Built by the DoD, TCP/IP has four layers. From its design, TCP/IP is no different than a scaled down version of OSI, which has seven layers. The four TCP/IP layers are:

- Network access

- Internet

- Host-to-host

- Process/application layer

The following table shows the correlation between the DoD model and the OSI model

OSI	DoD
Application	Process/Application
Presentation	
Session	
Transport	Host-to-host
Network	Internet
Data Link	Network Access
Physical	

Process/Application Layer

The process/application layer defines the requirements for application communication between different nodes on the network, and the specification guidelines for user interfaces. This layer deals with the services and applications that IP networks use, as discussed herein:

Telnet

The role of this protocol is to emulate terminals, and you will often come across forums where it is referred to as the chameleon protocol. Telnet allows someone using a remote client machine (telnet client) access to resources for a different machine (telnet server).

To do this, telnet makes it appear as though the telnet client is a terminal that is connected to the local network, in the process creating a virtual terminal and allowing interaction with the remote host.

One of the challenges of telnet is that it does not offer encryption or security. If you need security features during the remote session, telnet is replaced by secure shell (SSH).

File transfer protocol (FTP)

To understand how important FTP is to your network, consider the fact that without FTP you would not be able to transfer any files over an IP network. FTP is special because it doubles up as a protocol and a program. The difference lies in utility.

When using FTP as a program, it is run by users. On the other hand, as a protocol, FTP is used by applications. Through FTP you can also access files in different repositories and directories. Other than access, you can also move the files from one directory to another.

FTP is important for file management between hosts. However, you cannot use FTP to execute a remote file to run as a program. To use FTP you must have access to the necessary authentication details.

Secure File Transfer Protocol (SFTP)

You might be concerned about the security of a given network, and thus worried about transferring files across it. This concern is mitigated by SFTP. SFTP allows you to transfer files over an encrypted connection. The encryption is performed by SSH. Other than the aspect of encryption, SFTP performs the same role as FTP; access and transfer of files over different computers or IP networks.

Trivial File Transfer Protocol (TFTP)

TFTP is a very simple yet effective FTP version. It is ideal for people who already know what they are doing. To use TFTP, you probably know the file you are looking for and where it is located. TFTP is very fast, because it is not loaded with as many functions as FTP. You cannot browse a directory through TFTP. It is purely for sending and receiving files over a network.

Considering the fact that TFTP is a minimalist version of FTP, you are limited in the size of data blocks that you can transfer across it. Other than that, TFTP does not have any authentication protocols. Therefore, it is a rather insecure protocol, and as a result, not many sites use it.

Network File System (NFS)

In file sharing, NFS is a godsend. NFS specifically allows interoperability between different file systems. NFS apportions memory on different file systems so that you can still access, store and transfer files. A good example of this is when you connect to a network using a MacBook, but need to access files from someone who is running a Microsoft operating system on their computer. These are two dissimilar systems in that their file systems, security, name of file names, case sensitivity, and so forth are not the same. However, NFS makes it possible for both of you to access the same file with the indigenous parameters of your file system.

Simple Mail Transfer Protocol (SMTP)

SMTP is responsible for making sure you receive emails as soon as possible. The SMTP server is constantly running, refreshing and checking for new messages to your address. If any message is detected, it delivers the messages. SMTP works hand in hand with POP3. While SMTP is responsible for sending messages, POP3 receives them.

Post Office Protocol (POP)

The POP protocol simply acts as a warehouse for any incoming mails to your address. Immediately after you connect to a POP3 server, any messages that had been sent to you are downloaded. The interaction between the client and the POP server ends the moment the messages are downloaded and you can interact with them.

Internet Message Access Protocol Version 4 (IMAP4)

While POP3 has been effective over the years, standards are shifting, and most people are using IMAP4. One of the reasons why IMAP is considered a better upgrade is because it includes security features to protect you. Through IMAP, you have more control over the way you interact with the mails you receive.

Once you receive the email, you can interact with it without necessarily opening the email. IMAP allows you to peek inside the email, or read a part of it (the header). This way, you can choose whether you need to open and read it, or ignore it, or delete it altogether.

Users with a very active email address will also find IMAP very useful in that you can categorize the messages. You can sort them into groups, store them in a hierarchical order and so forth. IMAP allows you more control in the way you access your emails.

Transport Layer Security (TLS)

TLS is a cryptographic protocol that ensures your data is safe as you browse the internet. TLS, together with Secure Sockets Layer (SSL) ensures that all your internet activity is protected, whether you are sending an email, browsing the internet, or sending a fax message.

Secure Shell (SSH)

SSH helps you create a secure telnet session over a TCP/IP connection. Through SSH, you can securely sign into systems on the network, run applications remotely, and transfer files between networked systems. SSH is useful in that the connection is encrypted, protecting your internet activity.

Hypertext Transfer Protocol (HTTP)

HTTP is responsible for everything you do on the internet. HTTP manages all communications between web servers and browsers, to make sure that whenever you click on any link, you are directed to the correct resource irrespective of its or your location.

At the moment, a secure and advanced version of HTTP is in use, HTTPS – Secure Hypertext Transfer Protocol. Through HTTPS, your communication between the web server and browser is protected.

Secure Copy Protocol (SCP)

SCP builds on the flaws of FTP. While FTP allows you to transfer files across the network, it is not a very secure platform. The problem with FTP is that whenever you share files on the network, the user credentials are also shared. FTP does not have an encryption protocol in place, so your credentials are not safe and can easily be intercepted.

SCP uses SSH to protect your file transfers. Before files are transferred, SCP will ascertain that a connection exists between the recipient host and sender. SCP will also maintain the connection until the transfer is completed.

Domain Name Service (DNS)

The role of DNS is to resolve the internet names to the respective IP addresses. One of the perks of DNS is that it makes work easier. Look at a scenario where you decide to change your service provider. Since the website would move to a different domain, the IP address would also change. This can make work difficult for everyone else who needs to access your website. You might also forget the IP address. Because of DNS, you can change the IP address as many times as you want, but users will barely ever notice the difference. This is because the address they have memorized and relate to remains the same.

Host-to-host Layer

The host-to-host layer defines the protocols under which transmission service levels are set up for different applications. It is through this layer that end-to-end communication is performed, and at the same time, it ensures that the delivery of data is free of errors. Packet sequencing is performed at this layer, alongside maintaining the integrity of data.

The main reason why the Host-to-Host layer is important in your network is because it protects the process/application layer from the complexities that might be associated with your network. The Host-to-Host layer receives the data stream and processes the information. There are two important protocols that are responsible for operations in the Host-to-Host layer:

- Transmission control protocol (TCP)
- User datagram protocol (UDP)

58

Transmission Control Protocol (TCP)

The role of TCP is to collect chunks of information from applications and break the chunks into smaller segments. Each segment is assigned a number and sequence, so that the TCP at the destination can process them in the order in which they were segmented.

In such a communication process, the transmitting device will first establish a connection with the recipient. With an active connection, data is transferred, and upon completion, the virtual circuit established is torn down. TCP is a reliable and accurate full duplex protocol.

User Datagram Protocol (UDP)

UDP is a no-frills version of TCP. It is not resource intensive, but still does a commendable job when it comes to information transfer. UDP is therefore preferable when managing a network that would have otherwise been slowed down by a TCP connection.

One of the other instances where UDP comes in handy is when you need to transfer data whose reliability is not in question. If, for example, the authenticity of data was already managed in the process/application layer, you do not need TCP.

The network file system also manages reliability on its own, in the process making TCP redundant. The choice of UDP over TCP, however, rests with the app developer, not the end user who transfers files.

Another difference between UDP and TCP is that UDP does not sequence segmented data. The order in which the segments are received at the destination, therefore, does not matter. However, while TCP will follow up and retransmit segments that might not have been received at the destination, UDP does not. It is, therefore, an unreliable protocol.

The concept behind UDP is that each application has a unique reliability protocol built into it. Therefore, any information transferred through UDP must be credible. As a developer, therefore, you can make one of two choices; use UDP for very fast transfer, or TCP to ensure data reliability. Besides, UDP also doesn't check to establish a connection between the sender and recipient. No contact is made with the destination once the data is received.

The following table will help you tell apart UDP from TCP based on their inherent features:

UDP	TCP
Unreliable	Reliable
Connectionless	Connection-oriented
Not sequenced	Sequenced
Low resource requirements	Resource-intensive
No virtual circuit	Virtual circuit
No acknowledgment	Acknowledges receipt
No flow control	Uses windowing flow control

Port Numbers

UDP and TCP require port numbers to enable communication with the process/application layer. The reason for this is because they track all the chatter sent from or to the local host. The port numbers from an originating source are assigned by default by the source host. These numbers can only be in values of 1024 or higher.

Port numbers are used by TCP to act as identifiers for the destination and source of the sequenced segments. DNS will use both UDP and TCP. The choice of either will depend on the command the DNS is trying to execute.

Internet Layer

The internet layer sets the parameters for logical data packet transmission all over the network. Through this layer, hosts are assigned an IP address. The internet layer is also responsible for routing data packets to different networks.

In the DoD model, the internet layer exists for two reasons; creating a networking interface to the upper layers, and to route data. No other level performs the task of routing data packets. This layer also creates one interface through which the upper layers can be accessed.

The internet layer is important because, in its absence, developers would have to write so many versions of each application. It is through this layer that IP and other network access protocols interact and ensure that the applications run as they were written to. The internet layer is made of the following protocols:

Internet Protocol – IP

Everything about the internet layer is emboldened in IP. All the other internet layer protocols support IP. By design, IP stays aware of all the networks that share a connection online. This is possible because any device on a network has an assigned IP address.

IP monitors the destination address for data packets, and determines the best path to send the data packets based on the routing table. IP identifies devices on the network by determining the network to which the device belongs, and its ID. The network where a device belongs is identified by its logical or software address, while the network ID is the hardware address.

Any host device on a network must have an IP address, which is its logical ID. Through this address, the network has an easier time routing data packets from the host to the desired destination.

Internet Control Message Protocol – ICMP

ICMP is employed at the network layer, and serves several uses to support IP functions. IP uses ICMP for messaging services and managing the network. Messages carried through ICMP are transmitted in IP packets. The ICMP packets contain significant information that can be used by the host to determine specific problems affecting the network. In the event that the router is unable to transmit information, ICMP alerts the sender, informing them of the failed transmission.

Address Resolution Protocol – ARP

The ARP monitors the IP address to identify the hardware address of a host device. Basically what ARP does is to request the host device to respond with its hardware address. To do this, ARP reads the software address and translates it into a hardware address. In an ARP broadcast, the destination hardware address is listed in zeros in the ARP header, to ensure that all the devices that are connected to the network received the ARP broadcast.

Reverse Address Resolution Protocol – RARP

You might come across a diskless IP machine. It might not be possible to determine the IP address for this machine. However, you can identify the MAC address for this machine. RARP sends out data packets that include the MAC address of the machine, in the process requesting the IP address that is specifically assigned to it. This request is sent to a RARP server, which is a dedicated machine.

Proxy Address Resolution Protocol – PARP

Host devices on any network should never have more than one default gateway. The reasoning behind this is for contingency. In the event that the default gateway is down, you would have to manually set a default gateway. PARP eliminates this problem by making sure that the host machines can communicate with remote subnets without the need for a default gateway, or routing configuration.

One of the reasons why PARP comes in handy is because you can add it to one router on your network without interfering with the routing tables for any other routers on the same network. While PARP might be useful, it also brings about the problem of increased network traffic. To efficiently manage all the mappings, host devices must have a very large data table.

It is easy to consider PARP a protocol when in real sense, it is not. PARP is simply a service that is operated by routers in lieu of any other device on the network. More often than not, routers run PARP on behalf of PCs.

Network Access Layer

The network access layer oversees the exchange of data between the network and the host. It also oversees hardware addressing, in the process defining the protocols through which physical data transmission is conducted.

The network layer adds headers to the IP address. The address includes a protocol field with information about the origin of the segment, whether it is TCP or UDP. This is important to make sure that the segments are assigned to the right protocols at the transport layer when they arrive at their intended destination.

The network layer also uses ARP to identify the destination hardware address and determine whether the data packets can be transmitted on the LAN.

Chapter Seven

IP Addressing

To gain a better understanding of TCP/IP, it is imperative that you understand the concept of IP addressing. Every device on a network is assigned an IP address, which is their identifier. You might know the devices by the generic names that you might have labeled on them, but the most important identifier is the IP address. This is the address that the device uses to communicate with all the other devices on the network, and any other connection necessary on the internet.

To understand IP addressing better, there are some unique terminologies that you might come across from time to time. These terminologies will form the foundation of the knowledge you gain in IP addressing, and can also help you troubleshoot network problems from time to time. Let's look at some of the important ones:

- **Broadcast address**

  This is the address that hosts and applications use to communicate with all the other host devices in a given network. There are different types of broadcast addresses such as 255.255.255.255, and 10.0.0.0

- **Network address**

  A network address is used when a host device needs to send data packets to a remote network. Network addresses include 192.168.0.0 and 172.16.0.0

- **Bit**

  Bit refers to one digit. It can either be a 0 or a 1

- **Byte**

  Byte refers to 8 digits. However, depending on how it is used and for parity, there are instances where byte can be used to mean 7 digits.

Addressing Scheme

There are 32 bits of information stored in a single IP address. This information can be identified in four segments, each referred to as a byte. IP addresses can be deduced in any of the following ways:

- As a hexadecimal; FW.19.5T.24

- In binary form; 10101001.00011010.00110110.00111100

- As a dotted decimal; 192.168.34.25

While hexadecimal identifiers are not used as often as the other two, you might still come across some IP addresses that use hexadecimal identifiers, especially for unique programs and applications. One of the best illustrations of hexadecimal identifiers in use is the Windows registry.

A 32-bit IP address is often referred to as a hierarchical address or a structured address. This is different from a non-hierarchical address or a flat address. It is possible to use any of these addressing schemes. However, a hierarchical addressing scheme is preferred because of the fact that it allows as many addresses as 4.3 billion IP addresses.

The flat addressing scheme, on the other hand, is often castigated because of challenges in routing. In this regard, all IP addresses are similar. Because of this reason, it would be mandatory for each router on the internet to store the IP addresses of all the machines that connect to the internet. This creates a very big problem, and would make it impossible to enjoy efficient routing.

Hierarchical IP addressing, therefore, solves the problem experienced in flat addressing by introducing a tiered addressing scheme that identifies devices connected by the network, host and subnet, or the host and the network the host connects to.

Think of the hierarchical addressing scheme like your phone number. Each phone number is segmented into categories identifying the area code, the zone and finally the customer's unique phone number, which can be customized. Therefore, while flat addressing uses all the 32 bits as a unique identifier for the device, hierarchical addressing uses every part of the IP address to identify different components of the network.

Network addressing

Each network is identified by a unique number, the network address, also referred to as the network number. When you look at the IP addresses of all the devices on a network, you will realize that they all have the same network address in their IP address. Take this IP address, for example; 172.16.34.56.

The part designated 172.16 refers to the network address.

While every device shares the network address, the host address is unique. Every machine on the network has a unique host address. In our example above, the host address is 34.56.

Networks are often classed according to the size of the network, in terms of the number of hosts that are connected on the network. A small network that has a lot of hosts is a Class A network, while a large network with very few hosts is a Class C network.

The classification of host addresses depends on the class allocation of the network. There are three network classes, A, B, and C as shown in the table below:

	8 bits	8 bits	8 bits	8 bits
A	Network	Host	Host	Host
B	Network	Network	Host	Host
C	Network	Network	Network	Host

Class A

The characteristic of this network is such that the first byte is designated to the network address, then the rest of the bytes are allocated to the host address. As shown in the table above, this can be illustrated as follows:

network.host.host.host

If the IP address is 172.16.34.56, 172 refers to the network address, while the rest of the identifiers refer to the host address. You will also notice that all the devices connected to this network have their IP addresses starting with 172.

Class B

This network assigns the first two bytes to the network address, while the rest identify the host. The connotation is as follows:

network.network.host.host

Class C

This network assigns the first three bytes of the identifier to the network address, leaving only one byte for the host address as follows:

network.network.network.host

You might also come across special IP addresses, classified under Class D and Class E. These networks are identified as 224 and 255 respectively. Class D addresses fall in the range between 224 and 239, while Class E addresses fall between 240 and 255.

Take note that these are special IP addresses, and more often they will be used for research and scientific reasons. They are not very common. However, the range for these IP addresses is between 224.0.0.0 and 239.255.255.255.

Unique IP addresses

As you learn about IP addresses, you will come across a range of IP addresses that can never be assigned to any host by the network administrator. These are IP addresses that have a unique reason for their existence. The following is a brief explanation of some of them, and why they are special:

- The IP addresses is designated to 1s, like 255.255.255.255 – Such an address means that it broadcasts to hosts within the active network. This is also referred to as a limited broadcast, or an all 1s broadcast.

- The IP address is set to 0s – This addressing scheme is popular with Cisco. Cisco routers are set to default to 0s. By definition, this addressing can be interpreted to mean any network.

- All host addresses are 1s – This is used to identify all the hosts on a given network. Take the example of 172.16.34.56. This would mean all the hosts on the 172.16 network. It is pretty much a Class B network.

- All host addresses are 0s – This calls to a host on a given network. Simply put, it refers to the network address.

- 127.0.0.1 – This IP address is a special designation for loopback testing. The local host uses this address to send test packets to itself, without creating or using any traffic in the local network.

Private IP addresses

Private IP addresses are specifically limited to use within a private network. You cannot route these addresses on the internet. The idea behind such IP addresses is not just about offering unparalleled security, but it is also about saving space.

Private IP addresses are assigned to ISPs and some corporations, and some small home networks. The concept here is that some hosts barely need to get assigned a public IP address to access the internet. With a private IP address, they can connect to their networks and communicate with other hosts accordingly.

Anyone who needs a private IP address must use a Network Address Translation (NAT). NAT converts a private address in such a way that the user can still access the internet with it. In essence, this means that so many people could be using the same IP address to communicate on the internet, in the process saving up on a lot of space.

As a network administrator, how do you determine the best class of IP addresses to use? For a corporate network, it is always advisable to use Class A IP addresses. The reason behind this is that irrespective of the size of the network, a Class A network can be scaled up for growth and flexibility. Therefore, you can add and remove hosts to the network as, and when, necessary.

In the case of a home network, it is wise to use a Class C network. Class C networks are ideal for home networks because they are simple, easy to configure and understand. They are also easy to manage. A Class C network allows space for up to 254 hosts, which you will probably never exceed. A Class A network on the other hand, offers space for more than 65,500 networks, each of which can handle 254 hosts.

Internet Protocol Version 6 – IPv6

For the most part, you will come across IPv6 referred to as the internet protocol for the future. One of the reasons behind the creation of IPv6 was to mitigate IPv4 running out of IP addresses. Considering the fact that so many devices are already connected to the internet and have assigned IP addresses, it made sense to prepare for a future where IPv4 was exhausted.

One of the features behind IPv6 as a new age protocol is efficiency. This protocol is designed for full optimization and functionality that would allow users to go about their computing and networking needs without any concerns.

Each day more devices are built that must connect to a network. This is not a bad idea, considering that we live in an age where networking and connectivity are mandatory in many environments. Theoretically, IPv4 was designed to support up to 4.3 billion addresses. Of course not all of these addresses are in use. Of the 4.3 billion, roughly 200 million addresses can be assigned.

A conspicuous feature missing in IPv4 that is available in IPv6 is IPSec. IPSec offers end-to-end security. At the moment there is a lot of talk about end-to-end encryption. This is to make sure that all communication between the host and recipient is secure. In the age of the Internet of Things, there are so many entities that are keen on intercepting any form of communication. This explains one of the reasons why IPv6 is useful.

IPv4 is notorious for broadcasting storms. A broadcasting storm is a situation where you experience too much traffic on a network, crashing it in the process. Another problem with this scenario is that every single device on the network will suffer in the event of a broadcasting storm. The moment a broadcast is sent, each device must analyze the broadcast to determine whether it is meant for the device or not, in the process stopping anything else that the device was doing on the network.

To address the broadcast storm problem in IPv4, IPv6 uses multicast traffic. This is done in two ways; unicast or anycast. Unicast is no different from the way it has been implemented on IPv4. However, anycast is different. Communication through anycast is such that an address can be shared on more than one device. The idea behind this is to ensure that if traffic is diverted to any device that shares the address, it is routed to the closest host.

Types of addresses

Broadcasts are one of the key definitive features in IPv4. However, considering the fact that broadcasts are responsible for a lot of network inefficiencies, they were eliminated in IPv6. The following are the key methods of communication in IPv6:

- **Unicast**

  In this form of communication, all the data packets meant for a unicast address are sent to one interface. Considering the possibility of flooding the interface, the interface address can be shared with more than one device. This will help in balancing the traffic load.

- **Link local addresses**

  Link local addresses operate in the same way that IPv4 manages private addresses. These addresses are not designed for routing. The benefit of using link-local addresses is that you can use them to configure a temporary or random LAN whenever necessary, perhaps to host a meeting for some small task that does not need to be routed, but can still have access to local services and files.

- **Global unicast addresses**

Global unicast addresses are routable and public. They operate the same way in IPv6 as they do in IPv4.

- **Unique local addresses**

Unique local addresses are also built for non-routing needs. However, they are designed for global use. Considering the global approach, it is highly unlikely that you will ever come across any unique local address overlapping with another. Unique local addresses are designed to support communication on one site while at the same time allowing you to route the communication to a variety of LANs.

- **Anycast**

Anycast addresses will identify several interfaces to which they can communicate. However, they communicate by diverting packets to a single address. The address to which the packets are delivered is often the closest IPv6 address the packets encounter, considering the routing distance.

- **Multicast**

Multicast communication is a situation where data packets are transmitted to different interfaces, each of which is identified according to their multicast address. All multicast addresses in IPv6 must begin with FF.

Chapter Eight

Wireless Technologies

Wireless signals operate pretty much in the same way that ethernet hubs do. They support back and forth communication. These signals operate in the same frequency to receive and transmit data packets, hence such wireless technologies are half-duplex.

A Wireless LAN uses radio frequencies (RF) that are transmitted from an antenna. Considering how far these signals travel at times, they are prone to vulnerability. There are a lot of factors in the immediate environment that might also be responsible for interfering with the quality of network service delivery.

One of the possible ways of improving the network is to increase the transmission power. However, while increasing the transmission power might work, it also creates a new problem, opening up the network to the possibility of distortion. Besides, higher frequencies do not come cheap either.

The wireless specification 802.11 was created to support network freedom. Under this specification, you do not need licensing in most jurisdictions to operate a wireless network. Therefore, all devices that support wireless connection can communicate without necessarily having to force the administrator or user to create a complex wireless network.

Considering that wireless networks transmit data through radio frequencies, in some areas they are regulated by the same laws that monitor the operation of radio frequencies like AM and FM. The Federal Communications Commission (FCC) in the US oversees the use of wireless devices. In support, the Institute of Electrical and Electronics Engineers (IEEE) establishes the standards upon which the frequencies released by the FCC can be used.

For public use, the FCC allows 900 MHz, 2.4GHz and 5GHz. The first two are identified as the Industrial, Scientific and Medical bands (ISM) while the 5GHz band is Unlicensed National Information Infrastructure band (UNII).

Before you run a wireless network outside of these three bands, therefore, you must seek approval from the FCC. The 802.11b/g wireless network is one of the most commonly used all over the world today.

802.11

This network was the pioneer of WLAN, standardized at 1Mbps and 2Mbps. 802.11 is operated in the 2.4 GHz frequency. While it is popular, it was not until 802.11b was released that its uptake increased. There are many committees in the 802.11 standard, each of which serves a unique purpose.

Components of a wireless network

Wireless networks require fewer components compared to wired networks. Basically, all you need for your wireless network to operate effectively is a wireless NIC and an access point (AP). Once you understand how these two components work, you can install them easily and operate the network without any challenges.

Wireless Network Interface Card (NIC)

Each host must have a wireless network interface to connect to a wireless network. The role of a wireless network interface card is no different from that of a normal network interface card.

Access Point (AP)

You need a central component in the network to enable communication. For a wired network, this would be a switch or a hub. For a wireless network, you need a wireless access point. Most APs have at least two antennas to boost their communication range. They also have a port through which they connect to a wired network.

A wireless network must have some cable running through it. Most wireless networks are connected to a wired network through an AP. The AP bridges the two network types.

Wireless antenna

An antenna in a wireless network serves two roles. It can act as a receiver and a transmitter. At the moment there are two types of antennas you will come across in the market, a directional antenna or an omnidirectional antenna.

While directional antennas are point-to-point, omnidirectional antennas are point-to-multipoint. The directional antennas offer a wider range compared to the omnidirectional antennas in the same gain range. The reason for this is because all the power in a directional antenna is focused to one direction.

Perhaps the challenge of using a directional antenna is that you must be very accurate when positioning its communication points. For this reason, directional antennas are an ideal choice when setting up point-to-point connections, or bridging different access points.

Omnidirectional antennas are popular with APs because more often, clients want to access the network in different directions at any given time. A directional antenna would make this quite a challenge, because the client would have to position their access in one direction to enjoy access.

Setting up a wireless network

You can set up a wireless network in one of two ways. You can either use an ad hoc set up, or infrastructure mode.

Ad hoc setup

For this setup, the devices connected can communicate with one another without having to use an AP. This is what happens when you create an ad hoc wireless network on your laptop to communicate with other devices that can connect to it.

As long as you use the right settings, devices that are connected to the network can share files without any issues. When installing the network, one of the prompts will require you to choose whether you are using an ad hoc mode or infrastructure mode.

For this set up to work, make sure that your computers are within 90 meters of one another. Once they can detect one another, you can communicate and share files. The problem with an ad hot network is that it never scales well, and for this reason you should never use this in an organizational set up. This network is also prone to a lot of collisions. One of the reasons why ad hoc networks are no longer appealing today is because the cost of obtaining APs is very affordable, it does not make sense to run an ad hoc network.

Infrastructure mode

Infrastructure mode allows you to connect to a network, enjoying the benefits of a wired network without the unsightly cables. In this mode, the NIC communicates through an AP instead of directly to whichever device is on the network as is the case in an ad hoc setting.

All forms of communication between host devices on this network must pass through the AP. When connected to this network, all the hosts appear to the other devices on the network in the same way they appear on a wired network. Before you connect your client to on this mode, make sure you understand some of the basic concepts, especially security.

Factors to consider when installing a large wireless network

When connecting a large wireless network, you must adhere to specific design considerations. A lot of organizations today use mesh infrastructure. One of the reasons for this is because it is decentralized and dependable. Mesh infrastructure is also one of the most affordable

78

setups, so most organizations find it feasible. These networks are affordable because each host only needs to broadcast data packets as far as the nearest host.

In such a network, each host in the network is a repeater, so instead of one host struggling to transmit the data all over the network, it carries it to the next host who then passes it on and so forth until the data is transmitted to the intended recipient. A mesh interface, therefore, is a reasonable consideration especially when you are building a network over a difficult topography.

Mesh topology is implemented with several fail-safes in the form of redundancy connections between hosts. Since the design basically is built around making sure redundancies are a thing of the past, a mesh topology is perfect for a large institution or installation.

Mesh networks are highly reliable. Considering that each host on the network is connected to many other hosts, any one of these hosts dropping out of the network does not affect the system. Perhaps one of the hosts malfunctions or experiences a software challenge. Instead of data hanging, the other hosts on the network simply find an alternative route and continue transmitting the data packets. Anyone on the network will barely notice one of the hosts is missing.

Would you employ a mesh network on a home network? It sounds so good in theory, but in application, a mesh network is not ideal for a home network, or for any small organization that operates on a very tight budget.

Signal degradation

Whenever you are installing a wireless network, one of the things you have to worry about is signal degradation. All 802.11 networks use radio frequencies. With this in mind, the strength of the signal will be determined by and affected by a lot of factors, most of which you have no control over. A weak network is quite an unreliable network, and anyone who connects to it would be frustrated. The following are some of the reasons why you might have fluctuating wireless network signals:

- **Interference**

  Interference from outside will affect your network. As we mentioned earlier, the 802.11 protocol operates between 900MHz and 5GHz range. Given this consideration, there are so many sources that might cause interference as long as they exist within this range.

  Some of the causes of interference are in your vicinity, and include another wireless network, mobile phones, microwave appliances, and Bluetooth devices. Any device that uses a transmission frequency close to the frequency your 802.11 wireless network uses will interfere with the network.

- **Wireless network protocols**

  Which protocol did you use when installing the wireless network? We already know there are different protocols that exist under 802.11. Each of the protocols operate under a specific maximum frequency range. For example, an 802.11b protocol will conflict with an 802.11g protocol.

- **Barriers**

  Wherever you have a wireless network, always remember that barriers can affect the ability to transmit data on it. The signal will be weaker if it has to bypass a number of walls to get to the user. A wireless network with a range of around 100 feet might have the range drop to around 20 feet if there are so many walls within the office block. The thickness of the walls also impedes network access.

- **Distance**

  This one is pretty obvious. The further away you are from the wireless network, the weaker your signal will be. Most access points today are built with a range of 100 meters. To extend this range, you must use amplifiers.

Chapter Nine

Network Management Practices

Nothing comes easy. You must always have a plan for everything. Building a successful network to the point where it is up and running is not an easy task either. You must have a good plan. A good plan is one that considers contingency measures to ensure that in the event of any problem, you can troubleshoot the network.

Network management starts at the planning stage. During planning, you map out what the network should do, the goals you hope to achieve and your objectives. A plan allows you something to use for reference purposes especially when things are not working. This is where documentation comes in handy.

One of the most important things you must always have in the documentation is a clear statement of the baseline for network performance. From this baseline, you can evaluate performance to determine whether the network is performing at its peak or if you are lagging behind. Having a baseline for performance is useful in troubleshooting networks, because you know the limits of the network resources.

Importance of network documentation

For most networking experts, documentation is one of the most arduous processes you will ever complete. Most of the time you believe you already know what the network does, and how to fix it in the event of a problem. However, never underestimate the importance of documentation. The network documentation should be prepared and stored safely. For this, ensure you have an electronic copy of the documentation, which you can access easily and modify where applicable.

Other than an electronic copy, keep a hard copy printed and easily accessible. Ensure it is in a location where you can direct someone to obtain and use it in case you are not physically present to troubleshoot the network.

Finally, ensure you have another copy of the documentation kept in a storage facility away from the network. This should be an external storage facility such that the documentation can survive in the event that something tragic happens to the building that houses the network. Even with all the computing we are exposed to, it is still important to make sure you keep hard copies for the sake of contingencies.

There are three different groups in which network documentation can fit:

- Baseline documentation

- Schematics

- Procedures, policies, and regulations

Baseline documentation

A baseline is simply the basic performance level that you expect of the network or service when it is running in the expected environmental features and resource limits. An example of a baseline specification might indicate the number of processors needed to keep the server running at optimum performance, or the amount of data that passes through the server at peak hours. The idea of a baseline is to help you figure out at a glance, whether the network is performing effectively. In the case of a networking environment, baseline documentation will often include the following important elements:

- Memory

- Processor capacity

- Network adapter

- Storage facility (hard drive)

Once you have the network running, it is wise to determine the base performance of all the important services and sectors of the network. You might need to work with averages too. Do not take the first measurements you get from your initial assessment as the norm. Conduct tests on the network at different times, especially to compare peak and off-peak performance times.

You want to know how capable the network is to withstand the performance pressure. Knowledge of such information always comes in handy when troubleshooting a network or in the aftermath of a serious issue. It also helps you understand why some devices are operating the way they are, and what can be done to improve their performance.

Today you have access to a variety of network monitoring programs that can help you identify and monitor baselines. Developers have gone ahead and included monitoring software in the server operating systems, to help you identify the base performance level. Even after doing all this, you should never rest on your laurels. Always make sure you monitor the network and revisit the baselines regularly, say twice or thrice a year. This might also help you know how fast your systems are depreciating, and take appropriate measures to address the issue.

Schematics

Schematics give you a pictorial or diagrammatic explanation of the network. You can follow a process from the originating point to the terminating point, and identify a problem. A good schematic diagram will tell you what happens between points A and B, and why a given procedure cannot take place before another is completed.

Schematics will also be useful when you are discussing the prospect of widening your network. You get an artistic view of what the expanded network will look like, and whether it will meet your needs. At times subtle changes in the network result in overloading a given segment, while another consumes too many resources without relevant utility value.

You can create schematics from simple sketches to help you map the way forward. However, as the project evolves to an advanced stage, you would have to use special programs to draw a neat, elaborate, and presentable schematic diagram.

Whichever way you go about it, there are three different types of schematics that you can use when building a network:

- **Logical network diagram**

  A logical network diagram contains things like addressing schemes, specific configurations, applications, firewalls, and protocols. These are the factors that will combine to make your network logical and efficient. You must ensure you maintain and update the schematics diagrams as often as you do the same to the network.

- **Physical network diagram**

  A physical network diagram is a representation of all the paths to ensure the network is running efficiently. This diagram basically identifies the hardware elements of the network. It shows how the pieces come together to form a complete network.

  To create a good physical network diagram, assume you need to build the network afresh. What devices will you need? How will they be assembled? A good physical network diagram should address this.

  You should also consider any hardware or software upgrades in the network, and how they affect the setup. All this must be documented. In a situation where you are unable to draw anything, ensure your plan lists all the network devices. If you ever change anything in the network, make sure you follow through in the network diagram and make the same changes.

- **Wiring schematics**

  In as much as everyone is moving towards wireless connectivity, wired connections are still an important part of networking. Wired networking forms the backbone of all connections. Wiring schematics are useful, especially for troubleshooting. Color codes usually confuse a lot of people, especially in a network that you did not build from scratch. With the schematics, someone else can understand your connections, and solve the problem quickly.

  Another important reason why a wiring schematic is important is because in any network, each wire must be plugged into something. You should never have wires dangling or hanging without terminating somewhere. It saves your time when you know where each wire terminates, whether it should be the wall, a workstation, a hub, router or switch.

Procedures, policies, and regulations

Procedures, policies, and regulations are simply guidelines on how to run and manage the network. It comes down to following set guidelines. Adhering to procedures, policies, and regulations comes down to personal convictions.

Procedures give a clear description of the necessary steps you should follow in the event of something happening. Procedures tell you how to execute a policy. Say someone has been fired from the organization. In your role as a network administrator, the procedures elaborate on how to remove their privileged access credentials from the system because they are no longer friendly to the network. Remember that the human interface is usually the weakest link in the strongest and most secured network.

Some of the actions that are governed by procedures in most organizations include what to do in the following scenarios:

- A system audit

- Action plan in the event of an emergency

- Cause of action if the server crashes

- How to address issues arising to management

- How to assist someone who cannot access their accounts

Policies set the guidelines on how the network will operate, considering its configuration. Policies also create rules on how the network users should operate on it. Policies determine things like resource allocation on the network and network privileges.

Policies provide a guideline on how to do things. The following are some common scenarios where policies must guide your actions:

- Individuals who have access to the network and network resources

- How network resources are used

- Responsible use of company equipment

- Security protocols in place

- Frequency of backups

Procedures and policies are often backed by top management. The reason for this is because without their support, consequences for breaching procedures and policies might never be applied, much to the detriment of the organization.

Regulations refer to the rules that are set in the company or a governing agency like a government ministry. Regulations are rigid by design. You either follow them or don't. The consequences for not following regulations are dire, and depending on the governing body, could include jail time, losing your operating license, and so forth.

Regulations in networking and IT are guided by a code colloquially referred to as the CIA, which stands for confidentiality, integrity, and availability.

About confidentiality, data should only ever be accessed by those who are authorized to access it. On integrity, any data must be complete and accurate at the time you access it. On availability, those who are authorized to access the data must have access to it when they need it.

Information security is governed by many regulations. However, one of the most popular is the ISO/IEC 27002. This is an information security standard that was formerly referred to as ISO 17799. ISO/IEC 27002 is the brainchild of the International Organization for Standardization, and the International Electrotechnical Commission.

What you must always remember is that knowledge of the procedures, policies, and regulations for your organization and the industry in which you are licensed to practice networking is important. Compliance is mandatory, lest you find yourself in jail for forwarding an email to the wrong person.

Performance optimization

By now you understand why it is important to document every aspect of the network design to make sure it works according to plan. Once the network is running, you must monitor it and optimize it for peak performance in line with the baseline schematics.

One of the biggest mistakes that people make in networking is to assume that their networks are perfect. Every network will suffer a flaw at some point. Preparing for these flaws is what will save you time and resources. The best thing about monitoring your network is that you get to understand it better, and can optimize it and improve the performance.

Monitoring your network

There are several ways of keeping a close eye on the network. For most people, attention is given to resources like the network bandwidth. There are a lot of tools currently available in the market for this.

You also need to understand the health status of your network. You can determine this through the performance logs that are stored in the operating system. Performance logs help you determine the issues with your network, applications or services which might not be running as they should, and anything else that affects the network.

Most applications and programs today are built with event logs. These logs show you important information about the events and processes running on the network. If you are running a Windows server, the logs provide a lot of information, including the following:

- System – Includes all events from Windows system components, like services and drivers.

- Security – Includes information on sign-in attempts, whether they succeeded or not, and any possible security concern.

- Application – This is about the events listed by individual applications and programs. These logs are created by the developers of the said applications or programs.

Importance of optimizing network performance

Networks are important for so many reasons, one of the most important of which is communication. An optimized network enhances efficient communication. Today you need to ensure communication over your network is reliable. For this to happen, the network must be properly optimized for peak performance.

Optimizing the network means monitoring to identify flaws and address them. It involves a host of activities, including killing some processes on the server, sharing the server load with other devices on the network, installing the latest version of a program, or upgrading the hardware to the most recent model.

There are so many reasons why you must always strive to ensure the network is running smoothly. Here are some of the most important:

- **Uptime**

  Uptime refers to the duration of time the network is operational, and can be accessed by the relevant users. In principle, you should always strive to ensure more uptime. It might not be easy to achieve, but strive to ensure 99.99% uptime.

- **Resource-intensive applications**

  Some of the biggest challenges on any network are applications and programs that hog resources. Such applications are problematic for all other users. This explains why in organizations, network administrators go out of their way to banish and block torrent applications.

  Applications that consume a lot of bandwidth inconvenience everyone else on the network. Some of the notorious culprits for this problem include video applications and VoIP communication. Unless you have high-speed internet access, running these services on the network will always mean everyone else has to share the little bandwidth that remains.

- **Latency**

  Latency is a situation where your device hangs because the resources needed to perform the tasks you need it to are unavailable, or insufficient. Latency is the duration difference between the time you make a data request and the moment the request is delivered.

Procedures for optimizing network performance

When it comes to networking, bandwidth is one of the biggest resource challenges that network administrators have to handle. While it would be amazing working on a network that enjoys surplus bandwidth, this rarely happens. More often you are confronted with the reality of having to apportion bandwidth accordingly, and to police network users so you can limit bandwidth for specific roles, and probably throw those who abuse their bandwidth out of the network altogether.

Your role is to make sure that as much of the allocated bandwidth is available as possible, to meet the core needs of the network users as per the procedures, policies, and regulations within which your organization operates. The following are some procedures that you will learn to help you optimize the network accordingly:

- **Traffic shaping**

  Traffic shaping is one of the effective ways of managing the bandwidth on your network. What this does is that you set parameters for data packets. In these parameters, you will give priority to applications that meet the set criteria, and have their data packets prioritized over other data packets. It is basically about controlling traffic like police officers do. You slow down traffic for some applications so that you can decongest the network, and allow core functions to be performed. In the process, you clear the network backlog faster, and everyone else resumes normal operations.

  Bandwidth throttling is the technique behind traffic shaping. To do this, you make sure that some applications are unable to transmit data packets beyond a certain limit for a set duration of time.

- **Quality of Service**

  Under Quality of Service (QoS), your role is to make sure that the resources available are utilized accordingly, and everyone

93

on the network is able to enjoy the appropriate service quality without a hitch. To achieve the appropriate QoS, you should assign priority hierarchies for different network users according to their needs.

In each network you have users whose roles are core to the functions of the organization, and they need more bandwidth compared to those who need internet for basic services. By understanding the bandwidth requirements for each category of users, you can assign them network resources to meet their specific role requirements.

There are several ways of going about QoS. Each of these methods addresses some of the common problems that users have with organization bandwidth resources. The concerns you will address are as follows:

1. **Out of order delivery** – This problem arises when data packets use different paths to arrive at the intended destination in the network. The application on the terminating end is tasked with rearranging the packets in the correct order to deliver the intended message. The problem arises when the network experiences delays in rearranging the packets in the correct order, or if the packets are delivered out of order.

2. **Jitters** – Since each data packet might take a different route to be delivered to the intended recipient, it is possible that some packets might go through a network connection that is either too busy or relatively slower. It is this variation in the

delay that is referred to as jitter. Jitters pose a threat to real-time communication, especially over urgent matters.

3. **Delay** – There is always the likelihood that the data packets take a longer route to arrive at the destination, or they select a path that is already congested. Such delays often affect applications that are heavy on bandwidth usage, like VoIP.

4. **Error** – Errors happen when the data packets are interfered with while they are in transit. As a result of the interference, the packets are received in an unusable format. The recipient must then request the data to be retransmitted, which is a waste of time.

5. **Dropped packets** – Routers on the network might have to reject some data packets, especially when their buffers are stretched to capacity. On the other end, the recipient will be kept waiting for the data, which has to be retransmitted.

Through QoS, you can ensure that applications on the server are apportioned bandwidth according to their bit rate, so they work efficiently without delays. In case you manage a network that has surplus bandwidth, these are issues you might never have to worry about. On the other hand, if your network is limited, you must understand how to address each of these scenarios.

- **High availability**

High availability is an approach where you try to reduce the likelihood of downtime. In this process, you offer a guarantee that the network will enjoy a specific duration of uptime within a set time. High availability comes in handy when you manage the network for an organization that deals in important functions, like banking. You can also work with this when your organization is planning on something important, like perhaps live streaming an event. You make sure that through the duration of the event, you cannot have downtime.

- **Load balancing**

Load balancing is simply sharing the burden across the network. You analyze the load on the network and apportion it accordingly all over the network, so that the resources are shared equally and the burden is easier than it would have been if it were handled by a single entity on the network.

- **Fault tolerance**

Fault tolerance is having backup plans in a way that if any of the key elements of the network goes down, you will not lose access to the resources associated with that element. The easiest way to implement fault tolerance is to have several devices on the network that perform the service you are safeguarding. This way if any of them goes down, you still have the others to maintain network access while you try to get the other one sorted.

The easiest way to understand fault tolerance is like having separate hard drives on the network. Each of these drives is a clone of the main one. Therefore, if the main one has a problem, users can still access data from the mirror hard drives.

- **Caching engine**

  The concept of caching is to have a dataset that is a duplication of all the important pieces of the original data. Caches help you access everything faster. They speed up the load time because the device has knowledge of your usage patterns. A caching engine on your network is a unique database that keeps all the information that network users need to enable them to access their services online faster.

Chapter Ten

Network Standards and Protocols

K nowledge of network standards and protocols will always come in handy when troubleshooting network problems at any given time, irrespective of the network environment. A network protocol refers to the language in use by different systems that intend to communicate with each other. Systems must use the same protocol or language in order to communicate effectively.

A simple way of understanding this is through the language barrier you experience when speaking to someone who does not understand your language, and you do not understand theirs. It can be very frustrating. At times you are talking about the same thing, but because none of you understands the other, it becomes a problem.

In networking, the first step when troubleshooting problems is often to ensure that the communicating systems are all using the same protocol. If this is not the case, you will have problems. The following are the main protocols in use networking today:

- **NetBEUI**

- **IPX/SPX**

- **TCP/IP**

- **AppleTalk**

Understanding these protocols will help you solve most networking challenges and ensure the devices on the network are communicating as they should.

NetBEUI

NetBEUI refers to NetBIOS Extended User Interface. This protocol was designed by IBM, and is common in the earlier versions of DOS and Windows. Microsoft was one of the first adopters of this protocol.

NetBEUI is very common in small networks. The reasoning behind this is because NetBEUI is non-routable. A non-routable protocol refers to a situation where data is sent through the protocol, but the data cannot bypass the router to interact with any other network. Therefore, networks that use the NetBEUI protocol have the communication confined within the local LAN.

The non-routable feature of NetBEUI is one of the reasons why it is barely used today. Since packets cannot be routed on the NetBEUI, it is a simple and highly efficient protocol. It is one of the easiest protocols to configure and install in your network. More often, all you need is the name of the device and you are good to go.

NetBIOS mentioned above supports NetBEUI to enable connected devices to communicate on the network. NetBIOS (Network Basic Input/Output System) is the API (application programming interface) used when making network calls to remote systems. The NetBIOS protocol is included when setting up NetBEUI. NetBEUI needs NetBIOS to manage sessions and their functionality.

NetBIOS is also non-routable. However, it is possible to install it alongside the other protocols like TCP/IP to ensure that traffic can be shared across different networks. The following are the key communication modes for NetBIOS:

- **Datagram**

    Datagram mode is applicable in a situation where communication is needed, but without a connection or logging a session. NetBIOS also uses datagram mode for broadcasts. Unfortunately, Datagram offers no support for detecting or correcting errors. This is, therefore, the prerogative of the communicating application that uses NetBIOS.

- **Session**

    Session mode is necessary in a communication scenario that demands a connection, especially where NetBIOS is needed to establish the session with the communicating system. NetBIOS in this case, will also identify any errors in transmission, and at the same time retransmit any missing or corrupt data as a result of the errors.

    NetBIOS is not a transport protocol. Because of this reason, you cannot use it for routing. However, it depends on any of the transport protocols IPX/SPX, NetBEUI or TCP/IP for routing. To identify systems within the network, NetBIOS uses computer names (NetBIOS names). Such names cannot exceed 16 bytes for the name, and 1 byte for the NetBIOS suffix. For effective communication on the LAN, each NetBIOS computer name has to be unique.

IPX/SPX

IPX/SPX (*Internetwork Packet Exchange/Sequenced Packet Exchange*) is a unique protocol. It is a protocol suite. A protocol suite means that it contains more than one protocol. It is one of the most popular protocols in use with the earlier model NetWare networks. Current NetWare networks (5.0 and above) no longer use IPX/SPX. Most networks currently prefer TCP/IP. For the sake of awareness, you might come across IPX/SPX referred to as NetWare Link (NWLink).

The role of IPX in this protocol is to route information across a given network. Unlike NetBEUI, IPX is routable. For this reason, the base addressing scheme has to identify every system on your network, and the network the system is running on.

An administrator must first assign a network ID to each network. IPX identities have 8-character hexadecimal values, like (0SETQUID.). An authentic IPX address must have a network ID and a period (dot), followed by a 6-byte network card MAC address. The MAC address is a unique identification created for every network card. An example of an IPX address is 00-85-4G-8H-C2-25.

Considering the above explanation, the computer described above was connected to the network ID mentioned, the IPX network address will be 0SETQUID.00854G8HC225. Since a MAC address is already part of the address, you do not have to resolve it to communicate on the network. Therefore, communication on an IPX/SPX network is faster and more efficient compared to TCP/IP. TCP/IP does not resolve an IP address to your MAC address. One of the challenges you will experience with an IPX/SPX protocol is configuration. It is not as easy to configure as we had seen with NetBEUI. You must know about network numbers and frame types to configure this network. What are these?

A *network number* refers to the number that a Novell network segment is assigned. Network numbers have hexadecimal values, and contain no more than eight digits.

The *frame type* refers to the packet used by the network. You must ensure that all the systems running or connected to the network are configured to use the same frame type.

Assuming that you are connecting devices to SERVER3, which has an 802.2 frame type, you must set all the frame types to 802.2, otherwise none of the devices will communicate with SERVER3. Speaking of frame types, there are four main types:

- ETHERNET_II

- ETHERNET_SNAP

- 802.2

- 802.3

In case you are using a Microsoft device, the operating system is set to detect the frame type by default, allowing the operating system to automatically complete an IPX/SPX configuration. This makes work easier for you.

On the same note, if you are working on a network whose member devices have different frame types, all the devices that are configured to automatically complete an IPX/SPX configuration will default to 802.2.

IPX might be useful in routing packets, but one of its challenges other than being connectionless is unreliability. IPX is unreliable because it allows clients to send data packets to destinations, without the destination acknowledging receipt of the said packets. A connectionless protocol means that IPX does not log any session between the communicating clients before data transmission.

SPX mitigates the challenges raised about IPX. The SPX protocol ensures the packets are delivered. SPX is a protocol that is built around establishing connections. The role of SPX is to ensure that any packets that are yet to be received at the destination are resent.

AppleTalk

AppleTalk is a routable protocol that was built for Macintosh network environments. AppleTalk connects several systems to communicate in the network. Since introduction, AppleTalk has been implemented in two phases (*Phase 1 and Phase 2*). Most modern devices today use Phase 2.

- **Phase 1**

  The design of Phase 1 was specifically for very small network environments. Therefore, it is restricted to small workgroups, and only supports a few nodes on the network.

- **Phase 2**

  Phase 2 on the other hand, is built for a large network that can handle at least 200 hosts. Using Phase 2, you have support for extended networks, which means that you can assign a network segment to different network numbers.

TCP/IP

TCP/IP stands for *Transmission Control Protocol/Internet Protocol*. This is the most popular protocol in use today. TCP/IP is also a routable protocol. It is very popular because it is also the foundation protocol for the internet.

By design, TCP/IP can support networks and network environments that are not stable. TCP/IP was built for use by the US Department of Defense (DOD), and Defense Advanced Research Projects Agency (DARPA). Through TCP/IP, the relevant defense units were able to link systems all over the country that were not similar. To do this, TCP/IP is built with the capability to reroute packets.

TCP/IP has so far proven to be a very capable protocol. One of the reasons for this is because it can be used to connect dissimilar network environments. This explains why it became the foundation for the internet. However, this does not mean that it lacks flaws.

For all the benefits of TCP/IP, configuration and security are two of the major challenges that this protocol suffers. You need in-depth knowledge of IP addresses, default gateways, and subnet masks to configure and administer a TCP/IP network. Once you familiarize yourself with these elements, you will breeze through TCP/IP networking.

In terms of security, TCP/IP features an open design. This has opened it to security breaches, making it one of the most insecure protocols. To protect your network you must go out of your way and implement special technologies to guard your network, the systems connected to it and the network traffic.

Routing protocols

While discussing the main protocols, we have come across the terms non-routable and routable protocols. We have seen that TCP/IP, IPX/SPX and AppleTalk are routable protocols while NetBEUI is a non-routable protocol. What is the difference between these two types of protocols?

Routable is used to refer to a network where data packets from your network must pass through a router to be delivered to a different and remote network.

Non-routable protocol, on the other hand, is a situation where the protocol cannot allow the transferability of packets from one network to another. The reason behind this is because the protocol is built to be simple, and as such lacks the capability to acknowledge multiple networks.

An example of this is when the NetBEUI protocol uses NetBIOS naming to pass data across the network. However, NetBIOS names cannot be used to determine the network where the destination client belongs. On the other hand, an IPX/SPX or TCP/IP protocols include a network ID in their addresses, which can identify the destination network.

Command Line Tools

Since most people are using TCP/IP today, you should learn a few tricks to help you test your network for connectivity issues. For networking, there are many utilities that you can use to verify the TCP/IP function on your network or devices.

Traceroute (Tracert)

Ever sat down and wondered where the data packets go when you are browsing online? How do they get from your device to the destination? The answers to these questions are found in traceroute. The output of this command line shows you all the routers the TCP/IP packet goes through before it gets to the destination.

Tracert uses time-outs, time to live (TTL) and ICMP – internet control message protocol error messages to display this information. You can also use tracert to determine the router that might be causing you problems while troubleshooting a network issue.

Use tracert as a command prompt by entering tracert, space, the IP address or DNS name of the host. This command sends back a list of all the IP addresses and DNS names the packet travels through to reach the destination.

Tracert will also reveal the duration it takes for data packets to be transmitted in each step, through TTL. Tracert is useful when diagnosing a problem where a client is unable to reach a web server on the internet. It helps you determine whether the WAN link is working or if the server has malfunctioned.

In some cases, the command line might return an asterisk instead of the expected results. What this means is that the link you are investigating is too slow, or the router in question is very busy at that moment. It is also possible that the network administrator on that specific router might have disabled their ICMP protocol.

Ipconfig (ifconfig)

This command shows you the current TCP/IP configurations on the workstation. ipconfig returns a list of the default gateway, DNS configuration and IP address among other useful information. Since IPv6 is enabled in modern devices, ipconfig will also show this information.

When you have changed your network, it helps to know the new IP address your device is using. To do this, type *ipconfig /renew.*

Address Resolution Protocol (ARP)

ARP helps translate TCP/IP addresses to MAC addresses when you are running a broadcast. You use ARP when connected to an Ethernet network to determine the machine on the network that is using a specific IP address. When the requesting device receives the IP address, it adds it to its ARP table for future reference.

ping

Ping is a basic utility that allows you to determine whether you can connect to a host, or whether the host is responding. The ping syntax is as follows:

Ping IP address or hostname

There are so many options that you can use with the ping command, which will reveal different features about the workstation or the host.

nslookup

The nslookup utility helps you query a name server to identify the IP addresses to which specific names resolve. This is ideal especially when you are configuring a new workstation or server to access the internet.

The nslookup command helps you find out the unique features of a given domain name, and the servers that it connects to. It also shows the configuration of these servers.

Chapter Eleven

Mitigating Network Threats

There is nothing wrong with being paranoid about your network, or network security. In fact, paranoia might actually save you. Today networks are under threat from so many elements. There are people who just need access to your network resources because they can for fun, but others will want to steal important information. There is so much damage that someone can do to you when they gain access to your network.

Network security is something that most people barely take seriously, yet it might actually be the difference between life and death. A security breach can cripple the entire network, rendering you sitting ducks.

To be very honest, network security is as important as a basic need, and you should do your best to make sure you keep a clean, secure network. There are many security threats that you will learn about. Some have been around for years, others might come up in the future. Some threats simply evolve and become stronger, worse iterations of their former selves.

The secret to maintaining your network integrity in terms of security lies in mitigating risks. Disaster preparedness is something you should always work on. Even the strongest network is always at risk of a security threat.

Identifying threats

The dangers to your network are insane. There are so many risks out there that you would be foolhardy to ignore them, or assume that you have the most protected network. One tactic that works for a lot of organizations is to work with experts to try hacking the network from time to time, to gauge the level of security, and determine whether you need to do more.

Most people only recognize malware and viruses as the biggest risk in as far as network security is concerned. Indeed, an infection will ground you. However, there are so many other risks out there that can have just as damning an effect on your network.

Anyone who tries to gain unauthorized access to your network usually does so either for reconnaissance, or for destructive reasons. Some security breaches are so carefully crafted they can accomplish both. Security breaches are important because there is so much damage that can be done with the information accessed from your network.

Many people are currently paying the price for using an insecure network. Their private and personal data was stolen, and some of them were impersonated. You might end up being linked to a terror attack you had no idea about, because someone stole your identity and used it for such. Enough about the scary details though. Here are some of the common network security concerns that you will encounter from time to time as a network administrator:

- **Denial of service**

Denial of service attacks (DoS) block you from accessing the network or resources associated with the network. It can be done in so many ways. DoS attacks are common today, and they usually target large corporations.

The attackers can flood the organization website with too much traffic that the servers cannot handle, making it impossible for legitimate users to access the website.

- **Ping of death**

The ping of death is one of the common forms of DoS attacks. As you learned earlier, ping is a command line used to determine whether your device is communicating with IP requests and responding to them accordingly.

So what happens in the ping of death attack? To communicate, your device sends ICMP packets to a remote host to establish its availability. However, in a ping of death attack, the intruder will flood the remote host with ICMP packets. When this happens, they probably expect the remote host to be overwhelmed, and in the process it either hangs or keeps rebooting. Luckily today a lot of operating systems are designed with patches and security updates to protect them from such an attack.

- **Smurfs**

Forget about the tiny adorable blue fellows you have seen on TV. Smurf attacks are nowhere close to adorable. What smurf attacks do is that they keep flooding your network with spoofed ping broadcasts. Spoofing is using someone else's IP address.

How is a smurf attack executed? The attacker will spoof your IP address, and after that, direct a humongous number of pings to the broadcast addresses associated with your IP address. The router that receives the request will proceed to broadcast the pings on the network, assuming it is a normal broadcast request. From here, all the other hosts will pick up on the broadcast. Since they are all echoing a response to the IP address request, they create an echo. In a short while, you will have a nightmare on the network because each of the hosts on that network is trying to respond to the request.

Smurf attacks are more effective when they target a large network. They benefit from the economies of scale. Smurf attacks might be a thing of the past, but you can never rule out the possibility of occurring. There is always that one random hacker who decides to take an old school approach that no one would suspect. Most routers today are programmed in a way that they cannot broadcast data packets haphazardly.

- **Tribe flood network**

Tribe flood network attacks are very complex, and are commonly known as distributed denial of service attacks, DDoS. They are orchestrated when the attacker launches a series of DoS attacks from several sources, and all the attacks are directed towards a host of devices.

112

- **SYN flood attack**

  This is an attack where your server or device is flooded with a lot of requests that are meaningless. When attacked, your device struggles to process a lot of requests, yet they hold no value. An attacker initiates this process by sending a lot of SYN packets to your network.

  When the requests are delivered to your device, it attempts to respond to all of them. Within a short while, your network resources are depleted or stretched to capacity. At this point, any incoming requests will be rejected because your network is struggling to deal with a flood of SYN requests.

- **Virus**

  The funny thing about viral attacks is that they usually get a lot of media attention. A lot of people fall victim to these attacks before they realize they are affected. A virus is a simple program whose effect depends on the intention of the developer who coded it. It is not always easy to determine the motivation behind a virus, but it is wise to assume complete devastation. After all, anyone who gains unwarranted access to your devices is definitely up to no good.

  Some of the common reactions that have been reported of viral infections include devices going on a rebooting loop, wiping your entire hard drive clean, deleting some files, sending meaningless messages and emails to everyone in your contact list and so forth.

An interesting thing about viral infections is that they never replicate on their own. They depend on the user to do something to execute them. Something as simple as downloading a photo online could have dire ramifications on your network, if the photo has a virus hidden in it. Most viral infections target places where people frequent, like social networks. Once someone has it in their device, it spreads like wildfire.

File viruses are the most common, and there is a likelihood that you might have fallen victim at some point. These are viruses that are hidden in files that you share all the time. Since you trust the individual who shares the files, you will barely suspect a thing. Once you open the file, the virus executes and your problems begin.

Remember when we mentioned that viruses are often planned around places that people frequent? Well, most of them are created to hide in applications that you use all the time, like a spreadsheet or MS Word document. You might have enjoyed a presentation and asked the presenter to share the PowerPoint file with you for future reference. If the file was infected, you become a victim.

A file virus is written to affect an application or system file that is executable. For those who run Microsoft Windows operating systems, file viruses have extensions like *.exe* or *.dll*. Chances are high that you will ignore these files assuming that they are system files.

When you access the infected file, the virus is executed. The virus will load to the system memory, waiting for you to load a new application or program. The moment that happens, it infects that program and before you know it, you cannot do anything on the network.

A macro virus is a script that performs the intended hack without your knowledge. Unlike file viruses, you do not need to execute anything to initiate this virus. Macro viruses are common because they are some of the easiest scripts to write. Most of them are harmless, but you can never take chances.

A boot sector virus is one of the worst kinds of viruses that can affect your devices. This virus embeds itself into the master boot record. When the master boot record of your device is compromised, there is very little that you can do other than wiping out the entire hard drive and reinstalling the operating system.

This virus overwrites into the boot sector, preventing the operating system from identifying the boot sector or boot order. If you turn on your computer but it cannot boot, citing an absent hard drive, or an operating system not detected, chances are high that you might have a boot sector virus infection.

A multipartite virus affects both your files and the boot sector. This is one of the most dangerous infections, and you will almost certainly have to wipe out the hard drive. Some of these infections are so nefarious, they can stay for months without detection from the point of infection, and cause havoc later on when you least expect it.

Today a lot of companies have measures in place to prevent their networks and devices from such attacks. However, you can take additional measures to protect yourself. Install and constantly update your antivirus programs. Avoid websites and networks that are risky and notorious with viral infections. If you like to read tabloid news, you will constantly be a victim of viral infections.

- **Worms**

Worms operate like viruses. The problem with worms is that once you are infected, they spread randomly. You do not need to do anything. As long as worms are in your system, they can do as they please. Worms autonomously activate, operate, and destruct.

How attacks happen

Depending on their ultimate goal, each attacker will often have an action plan to get what they want. Some attackers will lure you over a duration of time, in the process learning as much as they can about you and your network, even without your knowledge before they pounce and execute their attack.

Attackers can interact with you in a very subtle form and you will rarely realize you are being targeted. Something as simple as a computer game is sufficient to allow them access to your network. Armed with the knowledge that someone out there is always trying to gain privileged access to your network, you must exercise caution.

A directed attack is an attack that is orchestrated by an attacker. This is someone who was looking for something specific, or who had a very specific reason for hacking your network. A directed attack is different from things like viruses, for example. A virus might be transmitted from one device to another by unwitting users. Viruses usually take advantage of a weak system and embed into the device. Some viruses clone and look like files you see or access all the time, so you cannot suspect them at all. Here are some of the most common network attacks that you might experience while managing a network:

- **Active X attack**

  These attacks are embedded onto small apps that you must install on your computer to allow you access to something specific. Some websites require you to install Java or Adobe plugins to play some media. These are the simple ways the attackers access your devices. Once you install the app, the program runs in the background without your knowledge, collecting information that is transmitted to the hacker's server.

  Hackers who use this technique can remotely access everything in your devices without your knowledge. This is a dangerous attack because someone who can see everything in your hard drive might as well store damning information or plant doctored evidence in your device.

- **Auto rooter**

  An auto rooter is an automated hack. Hackers who perform this rely on rootkits. This type of attack is common with hackers who want to spy on your network. Once affected, they have access to everything you do, and can monitor your device for as long as they need to.

117

- **IP spoofing**

An IP spoof is a situation where the attacker sends data packets, but instead of using their real source address, they use a fake one. More often your network will be susceptible because the IP address is spoofed to look like it is coming from a device within the network, when in a real sense the packets are originating from an alien IP address.

The problem with IP spoofing is that routers will identify the packets and treat them as normal requests within the network, because they can identify the IP address. The best way to deal with such an attack is to have a firewall in place.

There is a lot of privileged information on the internet today. Think about the number of people who shop online, the companies that store user credentials and information on the cloud and so forth. Data is the new gold, and everyone is trying to hack into some system to obtain useful data. Corporate espionage, for example, is one of the biggest black hat businesses. People are paid too much money to hack into a system and obtain specific data. Implementing firewalls on the networks is one of the best ways to avoid this problem.

- **Backdoor access**

A backdoor is a path created by a developer to allow them access to the program or app without going through the normal processes. Most developers create backdoors so that they can access these apps for different reasons. Some use this as a means of troubleshooting the app if normal processes fail and they cannot access them.

For hackers, backdoors allow them to invade the network. It is always advisable that you monitor and inspect the network as often as possible to detect backdoors. You should also conduct system audits frequently to make sure your network security is up to par with the present standards in network security.

Considering the current state of affairs in data security, most countries place a lot of emphasis on the need for system and network audits. You must do everything in your power to protect the networks you use, or you might be held liable if a data breach ends up with an inappropriate use of the data obtained.

- **Application layer attack**

An application layer attack exploits loopholes in some of the programs or applications that you use. Most of these attacks target apps and programs that require permissions, because they collect a lot of privileged information. Anyone who hacks into your system with such an attack will not just gain access to the system and devices, they will have access to an information goldmine.

- **Packet sniffing**

Packet sniffers are tools that network managers use to troubleshoot the network. They scour the network for problems. However, these same tools can also be used by hackers. Packet sniffers are commonly used by identity fraudsters to steal login credentials in the breached networks, and any other information that might be relevant to their cause.

- **Brute force**

In a brute force attack, the hacker runs a program on your network that logs into your server, for example. They gain account privileges and from here, use them for backdoor access. Later on they can access your network without needing passwords.

- **Network reconnaissance**

Network reconnaissance is simply spying on the network. The hackers take their time to obtain as much information as they can about your network before they pounce. They can scan network ports, or employ phishing techniques to get the information they need.

- **Password attack**

A password attack is an attack where the hacker pretends to be a valid user on the network, allowing them access to your resources and credentials. Password attacks can be initiated in so many ways. They can also be used alongside other attacks.

- **Man in the middle**

Man in the middle attacks take place when the hacker intercepts your communication. They read the data intercepted before it is delivered to the recipient. Internet service providers, credit and debit card swipe machines, and rogue ATM machine operators are commonly used for these attacks.

- **Trust exploits**

It has often been said that the weakest link in any security apparatus is the human interface. We tend to hold trust in high regard, and this is what brings down the entire system. You believe that someone cannot do something bad because you know them personally and they are not of that character. Unknown to you, they might have ulterior motives, or someone else might be using them without their knowledge. Trust exploits occur when a hacker manages to exploit the trust relationships that you have in the network.

- **Port redirection**

In this attack, the hacker uses a host machine that is already compromised. The compromised host machine is one that is friendly to your network. Since this machine already has privileges, the hacker uses it to generate traffic to the network, traffic packets that would normally be blocked by your firewall from getting into the network.

- **Phishing**

Phishing is one of the most sophisticated hacking attempts you can come across today. There is a good reason why it is referred to as social engineering. As we evolve with the networks, so do the tactics used to obtain privileged information by hackers. Phishing attacks require you to offer

121

information to the hacker that you would not offer in your right mind, but you do so without knowing it.

Majority of network administrators have taken steps to protect their networks from attacks. Hacking such networks is not easy. Instead of going through the trouble, hackers simply create something that looks legitimate and pass it on to the users. With this, they obtain all the information they need from you.

A good example of this is a hacker who wants to collect some information like identification details, date and place of birth, and so forth. Such a hacker can create a loan app, make it look legitimate and put it up in an app store. From there, they market the loan app properly and make sure they get the right attention.

Once you download this app, because perhaps you are looking for cheap loans with a bad credit score, you feed in all the important details you would provide the bank or any lender and wait for their feedback. You never get any feedback from the phishing hackers. They already have information like your full name, residential address, phone number, email address, and some even prompt you to create a password, which most people use the same password across all accounts.

Some phishing hackers even clone emails and make them appear look like they come from a legitimate source like a well-known government entity or bank. To avoid these, always make sure you use official links from websites you access. When you are in doubt, call the official contact details to find out the truth before you provide your information to hackers.

Some of the phishing attacks use keyloggers. Keyloggers can run in your system undetected. Today most keyloggers are built in such a way that they can send not just the key strokes, but some even capture screenshots and upload them to the hacker's server without your knowledge. Since you might be typing a lot on the keyboard, keyloggers can be programmed to capture only specific information like emails and passwords, phone numbers and so forth.

Protecting your network

While you are supposed to and can mitigate most, if not all of the network threats discussed, most network administrators cannot do this for different reasons. Some administrators assume certain risks are beyond their purview, and as a result, they do not give them the attention they require. To protect your network, you should perform the following:

- **Active detection**

    Active detection is a process where you scan your network all the time to detect intrusion. This should be an autonomous plan for any network administrator. Remember how you double-check your door before you leave, yet you have turned back and twisted the keys to the very end? The same applies to network security.

- **Passive detection**

    Passive detection practices require that you log all network activities and events on a file for review later on. One of the best examples of passive detection is installing CCTV cameras in the premise. You might not be watching the cameras all the time, but you are confident that they capture everything that transpires on the premises. If something is amiss, you can go back to the cameras later on and review. This is the same concept that applies with networks.

In the event of any network issue, you can always go back to the event logs and try to find out what might have happened.

- **Proactive protection**

Proactive protection is about preparing yourself for the worst possible scenario. You struggle to make sure that the network is incorrigible. All procedures and steps that you take to achieve this are part of proactive protection mechanisms. Proactive protection is about vigilance.

What can you do to protect your network from intrusion? Each organization must have some rules, regulations, procedures, or policies that guide its operations. When it comes to network security, nothing is ever too paranoid to be considered.

Make sure you perform a network audit as recommended by an external auditor. An audit examines your network to determine whether all the components are safe. While an internal auditor can perform the audit, you need an external editor for industry certified standard audits.

Ensure that you communicate the necessary security policies effectively, so that everyone is aware of their existence. This can be done in the form of a notification on the user devices. Something as simple as this "**UNAUTHORIZED ACCESS IS**

PROHIBITED, AND IS PUNISHABLE BY LAW" displayed clearly can act as a constant reminder to users that they must stay in check.

Any ports that are not in operation should be disabled. This way, guests in the office cannot use them. Someone might come in and plug their laptop into one of the free network ports, and in the process introduce a virus into the network without knowing it.

It is good practice to reset network passwords as frequently as possible. Some organizations perform these changes on a monthly basis, while others do it as frequently as weekly or even daily. The password you use when you come to work in the morning expires at the end of the workday when you sign out, and you get a new one when you sign in to the office in the morning.

Always make sure your network has firewalls running. Firewalls protect all the internet connections so that only those with warranted access can use the network resources. There are different firewall products in the market. Be sure to use one which suits your budget and is relevant to the size of your company.

Keep your antivirus programs updated to the latest version all the time. Run system checks frequently to weed out potential threats to the network. Most organizations perform security upholstering over the weekend when the office is not busy, so that when everyone reports to their desks on Monday morning, the systems are ready.

Chapter Twelve

Managing and Troubleshooting the Network

From time to time you will need to troubleshoot the network. You can have this done on schedule or on impulse, in response to an immediate threat. More often the need for troubleshooting catches you off guard. At times it is the very simple issues that make things difficult in the network. More often than not you worry about a serious problem, struggling to understand the cause, only to realize it was something simple, and perhaps all you needed was to reboot the network.

Network problems can overwhelm you. It gets worse when you have a problem at peak hours. Everyone on the network is unable to do their work until you sort out the problem. The pressure can be so intense, especially if you work in a fast-paced organization.

The first step in troubleshooting a network is to identify and narrow down the possibilities. The network issue might be caused by one of many reasons. Narrow them down and eliminate them one by one, especially if you cannot deduce an immediate cause.

For troubleshooting, no reason is ever too simple to be possible. Eliminate the possibility of a problem as a result of simple human errors. The following are the four key procedures that you should follow when troubleshooting a network concern:

- Check the network to ensure all the simple things are okay.

- Determine whether you have a software or hardware issue.

- Determine whether the issue is localized to the server or workstation.

- Find out the sectors in the network that are affected.

These four steps will help you eliminate possible causes one by one until you identify the problem, and fix it. Let's delve deeper into it.

Check the network to ensure all the simple things are okay

At times it is the simplest explanation that might solve your problem. Before you worry yourself about complex reasons for the network issue, try and eliminate any possibilities of a very small problem. Many are the times when someone will call you frantically that they are unable to access their account on the network, only to realize that they had the Caps Lock on.

While assessing the problem, ensure that the correct procedure is followed to access the network. Check to make sure the credentials are correct. Someone might be keying in the wrong details inadvertently. You'd be surprised the number of times people enter the wrong details and lock their accounts.

You can also create restrictions over the number of times users can sign into their devices. This alerts you when someone is struggling to access their accounts, and you can reach out and assist them accordingly. It might also come in handy and alert you when someone is trying to access a device they are not supposed to.

- **Login problems**

  In case your network problem is user-oriented, ensure their login credentials are correct. Where possible, try to sign into the account from a separate workstation. In case that works try it on the problematic workstation to rule out any other challenges.

  If all the possibilities mentioned do not work for you, go through the documentation for your network to determine whether there are any restrictions in place that you might not be aware of, and make sure the user is not in violation of any such restrictions.

- **Power connection**

  Check the power switch. Are all the devices that should be powered on running? There is always a risk that someone tripped on one of the cables and plugged it off the power source. You'd be surprised the number of times people complain about having a blank screen yet their computer is powered on, only to realize that the power cable to the screen was not plugged in correctly.

- **Collision and link lights**

  Check the collision light and the link lights. The collision light blinks amber in color. You should see it on the hubs or the ethernet network interface card. If this light is on, you have a collision on the network. For a very busy network, collisions are very common. However, if the light blinks frequently the collisions might be too much, affecting network traffic. Check to make sure the network interface card and any other network device are working properly, because one of them might have malfunctioned.

  The link light is green in color. If the link lights are on for the network interface card and the hub where the workstation is connected, this is a sign that communication between the hub and workstation is not interfered with.

- **Operator problems**

  Individual operators can have inhibitions that have nothing to do with the network, but lock them out and prevent them from accessing the network altogether. Perhaps the system you use is alien to the user. If they do not understand it, chances are high they will struggle to use it. Find out if the user has any challenges, and if so, walk them through it carefully so that they do not feel you undermine them or look down upon them.

  Explain to them why they are experiencing the problem. Be firm and make the user confident to reach out whenever they have a similar problem or any other. If you do not inspire confidence in the user, they may shy away from informing you of a problem, and instead attempt to solve them on their own, which only makes things worse.

Determine whether you have a software or hardware issue

Hardware problems can be extreme. One of the devices might have outlived its useful life. Hardware problems might also mean you need to plan for data recovery or retrieval if the hardware fails. Fixes for hardware problems involve replacing the devices, updating device drivers or tweaking the device settings.

Troubleshooting software problems depend on the nature of the issue at hand. Most programs today are operated on a subscription basis. Perhaps the subscription has expired and was not renewed in good time, hence you are locked out of the system, or your user privileges have been limited to free user account terms. In such a case, follow up with the relevant parties and pay the subscription fee to restore full access.

Remember that whether you are dealing with a hardware or software issues, you might need to back-up your data. Ensure you have sufficient space for this.

Determine whether the issue is localized to the server or workstation

Identifying the extent of the problem can help you know how severe it is. If it is a server problem, a lot of people will be affected, and you might have too much to deal with than if it was just one workstation.

For a workstation problem, you can try to sign into that account from a different workstation in the same work-group. If that works, you can trace all the necessary steps to fix the problem. Check the connections, the cable, the keyboard and so forth. Chances are high that the problem might be simple.

Find out the sectors in the network that are affected

Determining the sectors in the network that are affected by the problem is not going to be an easy task. There are many possibilities here. In case a lot of people on the network are affected, your network might be suffering from a network address conflict.

Check your TCP/IP settings to make sure that all IP addresses on the network are correct. The problem comes in when any two sectors in the network share a subnet address. This causes a duplication in IP errors, and it might take you a while to realize the problem. In case everyone on the network has the same problem, it could be an issue with a server to which they are all connected. This is an easy one to solve.

Check the cables

The way the network is set up could be causing you problems. If you have checked and realized everything else on the network is fine but the system is still down, you need to look at the cables. Ensure all the cables are connected to their appropriate ports. Patch cables between wall jacks and your workstations might need replacing. Most of the time people step on the cables, wheel over them with their chairs and so forth. If cables are run across the office floor, you might need to replace these, and probably consider a better way of running cables.

There are several cable issues that you might be experiencing. Most of them are basic, but they are the foundation of your network, so you have to know about them. Here are some of the cabling issues you might experience:

- **Interference**

  Computers are highly susceptible to signal interference. Radio transmitters and TV sets interfere with computers most of the time. These devices generate radio frequencies during transmission. To avoid this problem, ensure you use shielded network cables for the entire network.

- **Shorts**

  A short circuit might be caused by a physical fault in the cabling network. Today there are special tools that you can use to locate the short. More often than not, you will need to fix or replace the cable.

- **Collisions**

  If two devices on your network are communicating at the same time and on the same segment, there will be a collision. Collisions are possible if you are still using older ethernet networks, or hubs. Replace hubs in the workplace with switches where possible, because switches are intelligent and can help you prevent collisions on the network.

- **Echo**

  An echo is an open impedance mismatch. With cable testing equipment, you will know whether your cables are completing the circuit or not. Test to identify a bad connection. In case you experience an echo on all the wires at the same place, you might have a cut cable that needs replacing. Today some special testing equipment can show the exact location of a cut even if the cables are set behind the wall.

- **Attenuation**

Attenuation is a situation where the medium within which signals travel degrade the signal. All networks experience this problem. The risk of attenuation depends on how you lay the cable. Take copper, for example. You should amplify the network by a switch or a hub after every 100 meters. If you use fiber optic, however, you get a longer distance before the network is degraded. Consider your organization needs, and if possible, use fiber optic cables instead of copper. However, if you cannot afford to use fiber optic cables, have a hub or switch in place accordingly to prevent attenuation.

- **Cross talk**

Wires that are in proximity to one another experience cross talk when they transmit current. To reduce the risk of cross talk, paired wires are twisted and set at 90 degrees from one another. The tighter you have the wires twisted, the less crosstalk you will experience on the network.

Troubleshooting a wireless network

Most users appreciate wireless networks today, especially because they are easy to access from a wide range, depending on the settings. Wireless networks also take away the problem of running cables all

133

over the place. For network administrators, wireless networks might present one of the biggest challenges during troubleshooting.

First, wireless networks are synonymous with configuration problems. More often when you have a problem with the wireless connection, you have to go through the steps discussed above to make sure the hardware is okay, then you get into troubleshooting the network. The following are some of the common challenges you might experience with a wireless network:

- **Encryption challenges**

  Encryption is mandatory to protect all communication across a wireless network. Each network uses a unique encryption process. Some networks use WPA2, others use WEP and so forth. For the sake of security, make sure you use the best encryption protocol for your network. To make work easier, always make sure everyone on the network has their devices configured with the same encryption.

- **Interference**

  Wireless networks transmit data packets and signals through radio waves. For this reason, they are more susceptible to interference than the cable networks. A wireless network might suffer interference from a Bluetooth device attached to a computer in the office. This is prevalent especially when the object of interference is in close proximity to the network.

- **Channel problems**

A lot of wireless networks operate within the frequency range between 2.4 GHz and 5GHz. In between these frequencies, there are so many networks. Some channels are allocated more bandwidth than others, hence the reason why they are clearer and stable. Most of the time you will barely have an issue with channel configuration, unless someone intentionally or accidentally forces their device to use the wrong channel.

- **Mismatched ESSID**

A wireless device will always search for Service Set Identifiers (SSID) in close proximity. It might also search for an Extended Service Set Identifier (ESSID). If you are operating in a building where there are so many ESSIDs, you might experience interference especially when one of these has a stronger broadcast than what you own.

- **Frequency issues**

Each channel determines the frequency that the wireless devices must use. However, some devices allow you the freedom to set the device to a unique frequency. If you choose to configure the frequency manually, always remember to do the same for all the devices on the network. If you do not do that, the devices will not communicate. If you have too many devices to add onto the network, it is always safer to use the default setting.

- **Distance**

  The distance problem arises when the clients are too far from the network. One of the solutions here is to move the antenna or router as close to the clients as possible. If you are lucky to own a device with a very strong signal, you have to rethink the broadcast distance, because you might be susceptible to unwarranted access.

- **Antenna placement**

  The best setting for the wireless antenna is at the center of the wireless network, or as close to it as you can. However, in case this is not possible, you can also set an antenna far from the network, but connect a cable to it. Poor antenna placement translates to poor network performance, and in some cases, you might not even have network access at all.

- **Bounce**

  Bounce is popular in a wireless network that transmits signals over a wide area. To make sure that everyone has proper access to the network, it is advisable to install network reflectors or repeaters to boost the network. However, you should only do this if you can control the network signals. Otherwise, you will end up creating a very large network, which becomes difficult to manage, and also susceptible to hacks.

Procedure for troubleshooting a network

Having looked at all the possible ways of troubleshooting a network issue, the following are the appropriate steps you should follow:

1. **Gathering information**

You cannot solve a problem without knowing what it is all about. Collect as much information as you can about the network problem. How long has the problem persisted? What are the challenges users are experiencing? Which part of the internet or network are they unable to access? Ask all the questions, even those that might seem insignificant might point you in the right direction.

2. **Identify the affected sectors**

Whenever there is a network glitch, someone somewhere will be unable to do their work. Investigate to know who is affected, and how. During this process, if someone comes to you with a network problem, at times it might help to have them walk you through it from the beginning. You might just realize the cause of the problem in an instant.

3. **Scan for recent changes**

If you follow through the problem with the user and manage to recreate the problem as they described it, it means that you can track any changes that might have taken place on the network in light of their recent activities. Take note of the error messages displayed as they might also help you diagnose and solve the problem.

4. **Hypothesize the possible causes**

A hypothesis is about listing down the possible causes of the problem and then narrowing it down accurately to the right one. In some cases you might determine the problem immediately. However, in severe cases, some problems on the network are a culmination of so many other minor problems, so having a list of possible causes might help you diagnose and fix all the small ones as you build up to the larger issue.

5. **Does the problem warrant escalation?**

While you should be able to fix most networking problems on your own, there are situations that might be out of your hand, and require you to escalate the issue to someone with more experience dealing such. The sooner you realize you cannot handle the problem on your own and escalate it, the better it will be for you because you can bring in the experts in record time.

6. **Come up with a plan of action**

Having figured out the problem, communicate to the affected party that you are sorting it out. If necessary, walk them through the process. Each solution should have an immediate effect, or an expected effect. Ensure you are clear in this description, so that the user can alert you in case they notice something different from the baseline performance after you fix their problem.

7. **Monitor the results**

One of the biggest mistakes network administrators make is solving a problem and then assuming that everything else is okay. Each problem solution will always have a domino effect on something in the network. At times by solving one problem you might end up creating a larger problem. This is why you need to study the results to ensure that you can keep the rest of the network safe.

8. **Documentation**

If everything works just fine, remember to document the process, and the solution. Earlier on we had looked at the importance of documentation. It will come in handy later on when the same problem occurs somewhere else. In the documentation, include the possible conditions that might have caused the problem.

Remember to mention the software version in use. If you managed to reproduce the problem during testing, include this in the documentation. Mention all the solutions that you might have tried, and the effects, highlighting why you opted out of those solutions. Present the final solution that worked, and why you chose it as your best option.

Conclusion

Y̲ou are embarking on a journey that will get you so far, and change your life. The lessons you learn in this book will help you go a long way in your career as a networking expert. Once you are done reading this book, set aside some time and think about everything you have read. Each chapter offers useful information, and pointers that will guide you.

One of the important things you need in networking is a practice lab, or a computer on which you can try your hands on some of the lessons you learn in this book. The world of networking is advancing and keeps developing over time. Some conventions might change in a few years. With this in mind, therefore, try and make sure you have access to some practice material to help you stay abreast with technologies in networking.

If you have been in the corporate space for a long time, you will realize that staffing managers today focus more on applications over papers. You might have some really awesome papers but if you are unable to apply the knowledge learned and solve problems for the manager, they would not see the benefit of hiring you for the job.

There is so much you can learn about networks and how to manage them effectively. At the moment, network security is one of the biggest concerns that a lot of organizations grapple with. You are expected to know how to deal with this. When hired, the decision makers in your organization believe that you have what it takes to protect and safeguard their network resources.

The beauty of computing today is that there is so much evolution taking place. Things change so fast, yet somehow they remain the same. With in-depth knowledge of CompTIA Network+ you learn important lessons that will help you advance and evolve with technological advances as they happen.

CompTIA Network+ prepares you not just by teaching you the necessary information you need to pass the exams, but also by showing you the hands-on approach to solving problems.

Made in the USA
Las Vegas, NV
27 January 2024

84992906R00085